Towards Re-Enchantment

PLACE AND ITS MEANINGS

Towards Re-Enchantment

Edited by Gareth Evans and Di Robson

A
RTEVENTS

This edition first published in 2010 by
Artevents, 107 Mayola Road, London E5 0RG
www.artevents.info

Collection © Artevents, 2010

Individual essays, poems, illustrations and photographs are
© the named authors, artists and photographers, 2010.

The moral right of the writers and artists named to be identified
as the authors of their work has been asserted in accordance with
the Copyrights, Designs and Patents Act of 1988.

All rights reserved. No part of this publication may be reproduced,
stored in a retrieval system, or transported in any form by any means,
electronic, mechanical, photocopying, recording or otherwise, without
the prior permission in writing of both the copyright owners and the
above publisher of this book.

ISBN: 978-0-9549848-1-6

A catalogue record for this book is available from the British Library.

Designed by Fraser Muggeridge studio
Printed by Cassochrome, Belgium

Published for *The Re-Enchantment*, a national arts project exploring
our relationships to place, July 2010 – June 2011.

The Re-Enchantment is core-funded by the Paul Hamlyn Foundation's
Breakthrough Fund Award (www.phf.org.uk) and supported by
the National Lottery through Arts Council England
(www.artscouncil.org.uk).

The Re-Enchantment   Paul Hamlyn Foundation

Contents

9	*Tillydrone Motte* by Robin Robertson	SEATON PARK
13	*Water Walks* by Iain Sinclair	SPRINGFIELD PARK
29	*On the Virtues of Dis-Enchantment* by Richard Mabey	NORFOLK
41	*May Morn* by Jane Rendell	'MOSS GREEN'
61	*East of Eden* by Ken Worpole	ESSEX
83	*Votives to St. Wite* by Elisabeth Bletsoe	WHITCHURCH CANONICORUM
91	*The Grave of Dafydd* by Jay Griffiths	YSTRAD FFLUR
105	*Hevenyssh* by Lavinia Greenlaw	HOLKHAM
107	*A Counter-Desecration Phrasebook* by Robert Macfarlane	ISLE OF LEWIS
133	*Crow Meadow* by Alice Oswald	ASHPRINGTON
135	*On Rona* by Kathleen Jamie	RONA

For Sukhdev Sandhu

SEATON PARK, ABERDEEN

Tillydrone Motte

by Robin Robertson

I spent my childhood here on this highest edge,
this hill, in this park: my garden
spread out for me two hundred feet below,
the Don coursing through it, out towards the sea.
Fifteen years in every kind of light and weather:
my castle-keep, watchtower,
anchorite's cell, my solitary
proving ground, a vast sounding-board
here amongst the gorse and seabirds.

As the river-terraces below me filled with cloud
I stood over it all, making a ghost, a brocken spectre,
trying to cast the shadow of a man.

I knew all the places to disappear, to go
where you couldn't be seen from the path:
the pillbox, the tree-house, that secret beach
and hidden above it, the charmed wood. I knew
where the hawthorn tree stands,
bent and fixed like blown smoke,
the sun skimmering in the twist of the river water,
the rough hand of the sea-wind in the elms
and sycamores, the soft courtesy of snow.
I knew where to find the cloaked heron,
the cormorant clergy, where I once saw
the swan in the rapids with the Don in spate,
knew the names of the brothers

that drowned there, at the mill turn
– the Crook of Don – where the river tightens in,
where sweetwater meets the brine reaches. I knew
how it came down through the braes and weirs
to the green sluice under the hill, to coast
its way past Walker's Haugh and Kettock's Mill
to the Devil's Rock and the Lovers' Loup, drawing
deep through Tam's Hole and the Pot, over
the Black Neuk of the Brig o' Balgownie
where the river rests before the last pull
through the machair and out
to the sea beyond.

A distant smatter of applause and, seconds later,
I see the flock lifting, down in the valley,
losing itself in the far pines.

What I didn't know was this:
that there would come a time when I would find
the trees unclimbable, the river too fast to ford,
that I would learn it wasn't a motte at all
– this thrown mound where I went to be born –
but a Bronze Age burial cairn,
and not Tillydrone either
– this place where I stood my flensed cross –
but *tulach draighionn*, which means,
and has always meant, 'the hill of thorns'.

---

brocken spectre: (German *Brockengespenst*), also called 'brocken bow' or 'mountain spectre', the apparently huge, magnified shadow thrown by a climber on high ground looking downwards into mist or cloud with a low sun behind. The head of the figure is often surrounded by the glowing halo-like rings of a 'glory': rings of coloured, diffracted light.
tulach draighionn: (Gaelic) pronounced *tooluch dryun*

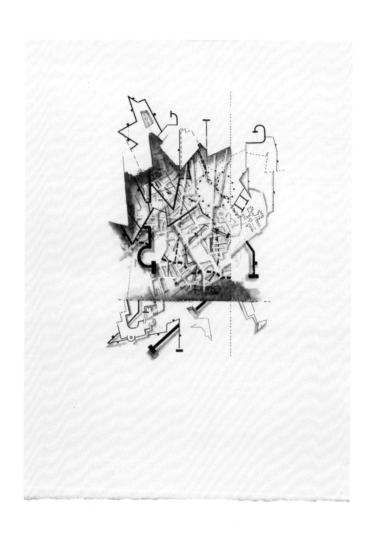

SPRINGFIELD PARK, UPPER CLAPTON, LONDON

Water Walks

by Iain Sinclair

What took me by surprise, coming back after so many months, was the Hasidic family, male of course, on the wrong side of the river. It was a thing, even in a period of soul-shredding development, quite unprecedented, and therefore worth recording. Not to the extent of risking a photograph, that response was illegitimate and unrequired, but at least making a small, illegible entry in my red notebook. 'They look at water.' The man in the black hat occupying a bench, his back to the marshes, and his two sons, restless, but staying inside the bounds of paternal authority. Until he draws them close, within his reach, to guide their attention, for a moment, to the river, and to the fact of the park, now on the other bank, facing them; a view, a framed quotation, and no longer a privileged shelf from which to indulge that hazy, incoherent spread of landscape, between the crowded marina and the low hills of Epping Forest. Not our business. English melancholy and its deep shadows.

Springfield Park, Upper Clapton, is distinguished by a geology that teachers and sponsored signboards persist in calling 'unique'. They want, quite reasonably, to explain the attraction, the mysterious grip a single visit can impose on random excursionists. There always was, and you find the device repeated in metropolitan fiction, before the First War, a dream of the good place, beyond the labyrinth, the dirt and noise, the exhaustion of repetitive labour, poor wages, narrow horizons. And there were other reasons too, apart from prison visits or relatives extinguished in suburban asylums, for taking public transport, the omnibus, tram or train: that *rus in urbe* residue, a memory-rind of meadows, spring flowers, blossom, birdsong. Within the grim stone canyons, blackened lungs and lips, a sudden shift out of place and time can be achieved. This hillside. The view of water.

Special holiday trams ran from Whitechapel and Spitalfields to Upper Clapton, depositing new and second-generation immigrants in a tidy park, which had been opened to the public in 1905 by the London County Council. A journey away from the ghetto, where, coming ashore disorientated, they had been left to fend for themselves. After a steady ascent in the crowded tram, molecules jolted and rearranged in transit, they step down, dazed and excited, into a fable, an idealised form, manifested transcendence; while understanding, all too well, that they must, at the end of a few brief hours, squeeze back into tighter skins. And so it goes on, generation after generation, in the novels of Alexander Baron, Roland Camberton, the routines of Harold Pinter, that conviction: how it is possible, even necessary, to escape, on a summer evening, at whim, to the marshes and the Lea Valley corridor, to retain that potentiality. Springfield Park was a conceptual space that was also a room without a ceiling, curtained with trees, box hedges closed around formal benches, a carpet of spongy grass. You do not see the timber yard around the bend. Nor hear the ugly talk in the riverside pub with the union flag. The railway, at a safe distance, is a picture in a child's alphabet book.

The photograph that survives from the opening day, more than a hundred years ago, is of a group of men, eleven of them, eight moustaches, one beard, a team: 'Park Keepers and Constabulary'. Arranged hard against an old wall. Badges of office fixed to bowler hats, pointed helmets. Waistcoats, heavy boots. 33½ acres of landscaped ground, the extended gardens of three villas, given over, under terms, to a respectful public, admitted under sufferance. They will be kept off the beds, the regimented paths, brought around the pond to the brow of the hill, the agreed position from which they will gasp in admiration at a staged panorama. A speeding cut of cloud. Like ducking your head, eyes shut, into a basin of cold water: and then staring straight out of an attic window at the morning sky.

From those benches, you do not turn back to London, nor do you anticipate the path out, to Waltham Abbey and Hertford. You are no Viking, no invader. The constabulary are recruited from working men, not unlike yourself, but not quite the same: Irish, Scots, back from the colonies, from war. They prefer it if you keep moving, no wild gesticulations, no excessive enthusiasm, no dancing. Three men in uniform per acre. They don't know, they have absolutely no sense of how soon they will disappear, faster than the original houses set here on the ridge, to be apart from Lower Clapton, in a kind of countryside, staring over and *across*; in such a way that middle ground becomes an ocean, shifting and fixed, a loose assertion of routes untaken, a prompt to subtle meditation.

The pastoral idyll is a sham, but a true sham; before the villas of the potentates, the ones who took a pride in walking down to their offices and counting-houses in the City, there were industries exploiting natural resources. Brickmaking, gravel extraction. George Baker's dye works. William Burch's calico printing operation. An ancient tree trunk, laid across several barges, made its stately progress down the Lea to Latham's timber yard. In 1855 these activities were visible, you could smell them. By 1870, even as London pushed out, speculative development spreading over market gardens and farmland, factories on the high ridge gave way to rusticated mansions. The old mooring place, Giles Dock, would be confronted by a future marina, narrowboats of libertarians avoiding Margaret Thatcher's punitive poll tax. There are 69 varieties of tree, left over from private estates, still to be found in Springfield Park. The essence of the enclosure is that it protects its own legend, its boasted singularity. The way that mythic ice ages can be accessed from the evidence of the ground, the bounce in the step on the thin layer of grass over sand and gravel, the fine deposits of brickearth from which white mansions assembled themselves. Before their time was up, villas like the ones found in Conan Doyle were demolished, disassembled, or converted into municipal tea rooms, convenience stations for bird-spotters and dog walkers. A hum of European languages from the benches.

And how prospects of river and marshes are laid out like an Open University lecture: rainfall draining through terraces of sand and gravel until the subterranean torrent reaches that impermeable coat of London clay. Beside the tennis courts, a spring line. Water seeping and sloshing from the ground, trickling downhill, streams and rivulets into the Lea. Springfield sands are known to geologists as the 'Hackney Terrace', suggesting already a site of strolling excursionism, promenade. The clay hump is older by fifty million years: crocodile-coloured, torpid, viscous, unforgiving. A layer absorbing and abolishing memory. Water clogs the football pitches where Orthodox boys, ringlets, white shirts, black waistcoats, stagger about in Sunday afternoon abandon. A former punk, a ruined dandy who grew up with various music business luminaries around Stamford Hill, told me that they came to Springfield Park to mooch and to play spot the yock, identifying the rare gentiles who invaded their territory.

What is it about this place that makes it worth invading? I was reading a discursive chapter, in a translated novel, in which a man and a woman, through relentless paragraphs, circle around the exclusion of narrative, any obvious forward impetus, but in which the author directs our attention, fleetingly, to one detail: a ladder in the young woman's tights, as it creeps towards her boots, climbs under her rising skirt. That naggingly present motif, among the acres of convoluted prose, keeps you going.

It doesn't take much. Springfield Park operates in a similar fashion on the clotted narrative of East London; but where the surrounding borough is all movement, drama, noise, the park is a still point, husbanding its pathology, offering those diagonal paths, ambles around ponds and copses, before the terrace, the compulsory viewpoint.

A quietly eroticised pleasuring of the senses: that steep, safe drop to the spring line, down which children love to run and tumble. Benjamin Clarke, a medical man and local historian, came here before the enclosure had been offered to the public at large. *Glimpses of Ancient Hackney and Stoke Newington*, published 1892–93, records, in episodes that read like letters to a banished friend, Clarke's speculative walks through the territory.

> 'We tread along still higher ground, and our terrace-line culminates in the beautifully swelling plateau forming the grounds of Mr. Bros – well named "Springfield" – Upper Clapton, and above Morris' Ferry.'

Like so many others, in the generations that followed him, Clarke believed that accidental evidence could always be found to justify his own obsession with the magic of place.

> 'Here, in 1814, were discovered all the marks of a Roman cemetery. A coffin of hewn stone was found six feet under ground, and on the slope of the land, sixty feet above the marsh from which it rises, in 1837, another coffin was found near the former, and at the same depth – they were lying north and south... We may fairly conjecture that on this rising ground, most beautifully and strategically situated, may have stood a Roman villa – part dwelling and part fortress or watch-tower... May I here venture to suggest to any who may come after me – to those who in years to come shall witness the still further advances of the insatiable builder – that whenever this lovely oasis in our

brick-built wilderness shall come under the same curse, all excavations be carried out with as much watchfulness and care as possible, that thus additional light may be thrown on my native parish, Hackney…'.

To renew ourselves, to revive the oldest parts of ourselves, against present annoyances and stupidities, we groove out certain routes and walks, bringing rewards, views, visions, cafés, pubs, parks. Stitching water into our sides, tramping and floating, noticing, forgetting, seeing again, is a simple human requirement. From the start of my life in Hackney, I explored the canal system, and beyond that, the River Lea. Springfield Park, and the café beside the boathouse, became the natural conclusion to a morning session, to the plotting of a story or script. The trick was to delete internal projections and fantasies, mental trailers that act as a nuisance filter between world and self, and to empty that space until landscape flowed through, freely and without editorial interference. We must become the becoming, alert not alarmed, walking just far enough for the process to work. The instinct goes back to Dr Clarke composing his reports on the hoof, to Pinter striding across from Lower Clapton, from hot argument, the theatre in his skull, to the solitude, the big skies of the marshes.

Now the café is busy, loud with new cyclists, map readers, oarsmen, nature bureaucrats, legacy technicians. Springfield Park is a hub on the cusp of grand project imagineering. In former times, when I exploited it as a staging post where, after a morning's walk, I would revise the story-in-progress, over coffee and a bacon sandwich, there might be one other customer, a gardener or a waterman. After scribbling a few notes, doodling frames for a film that would never happen, I would go into the park, across the slanting path, to the terrace and the hedged alcoves, to look across at Epping Forest. And to think for a moment about that other Springfield, one of the lodges of the asylum run by Matthew Allen, where the poet John Clare was kept before his brutal pilgrimage up the Great North Road.

Making yourself ready to accept the dictation of place is the first requirement: and then the unexpected, that wished-for second consciousness, will happen. Riverbanks, like the roadside verges so memorably recalled by Clare in the posthumous seizure of a feverish memoir of his return to Northborough, are peopled with messengers, angels of inspiration disguised as itinerant farm labourers, gossiping women on a village street, a forgotten wife and son on a borrowed cart. The effort of the thing, the dream of the walk, is exclusion, winnowing the deluge of impressions, sights, signals, sounds, to essence. On my most recent return to Springfield Park, a commission to produce a text of 900 characters (including spaces), the challenge of what to ignore was extreme. Leaving the camera at home was a start, making more room for those messengers, manifestations of enchantment, to reveal themselves. But my notes, prompted by incidents that seemed to contain the unique flavour of this particular outing, ran to several thousand words. There were those slowly circling cyclists, talking talking talking, on their phones, describing intricate patterns. And the voices heard on the towpath, such animation: German, Russian, Spanish. And the giant portraits of former inmates in a LCC block facing imminent demolition. And the solitary Muscovy duck edging around a floating tree on which a pair of aggressive coots had made their nest.

And that extraordinary moment when water cascaded over the path, near the Olympic Stadium, into the Lea. I took the effect for one of the more ambitious and successful grand project interventions, a beautifully charged metaphor, a waterfall as wide as Niagara turning the footpath into a vertical river. But I was wrong, burst Victorian pipes damaged by intemperate and hurried land piracy. The blocked songline, the artificial barriers, the Gurkhas employed as security guards:

frustrations defining a sorry era of indefinitely postponed enlightenment. A Chinese man, a jogger soaked in sweat, told me that he had been coming this way for 21 years, and had never known such a division between rich and poor. A section of the canal had been drained for cosmetic improvement, the loose change of an imploded economy, and a yellow tractor dredged through the puddled mud and filth, the shopping trolleys and traffic cones that are part of a submerged eco-system.

These incidents could be arranged to form a pattern, the armature of a narrative; or they could stand, without embellishment, as a list, a fragment with no beginning and no end. I dodged around that day's messenger spirit, without noticing him, because I was closing on Springfield Park and the desired café. I had a diary film sequence from years ago, half-remembered, half-mythologised, as a kind of resolution to my essay in minimalism. Outside the side window of the café was the sharp V of a hedged garden, a scrap of turf accessible through the door of the steamy kitchen. I was waiting for my coffee, with its creamy meniscus, to cool. I noticed the sleek fur hat of an Orthodox man, a black beaver, moving along the top of the hedge, as he walked away from the river. And, at the same moment, invisible to him, his nest of thoughts and obsessions, there appeared a solid woman, dressed only in a short blue apron, who came out of the open kitchen door, into the tight garden, to stretch and to smoke, her naked back to me. The effect was so painterly: dappled skin tones, her relief at being in the air, away from the heat, and then the heavy, wet-look fur of the hat, the bulky outline of the man in the black coat.

The drama of this non-event – hat, woman, watcher at table – is an improper conclusion; more like the start of another tale. It is self-sufficient, requiring no additional commentary. The real messenger, of this episode, is a blind man in a yellow tabard, leashed to contradictory dogs, testing the path with a long white stick or wand. The dogs remind me of the two empty plinths in Victoria Park, from which, yet again, the twin canine sculptures known at the Dogs of Alcibiades have been removed for refurbishment. There was nothing more to be said about this man, beyond the way he advanced, with such certainty, such a sweeping and probing of the path, on the blue fence of the Olympic zone.

When I returned home, there was an email from Rachel Lichtenstein, in which she reported on an interview with a woman met at a bookshop reading. Rachel had a gift for identifying and drawing out messengers of her own. 'She now lives on the Essex-London borders,' she wrote. 'When I arrived she took me out to her garden, which she told me once backed onto Claybury Hospital, where she worked, in the Sixties, in the library. She told me terrible stories about women being incarcerated for being single mothers and a blind man sharing a room with mentally ill patients.'

Stamford Hill in the rain. See-through hoods over the black trilbies of Orthodox Jewish men. Long black coats scurrying, with purpose, ballasted by plastic-protected bags, large enough to be constantly shifted from hand to hand. Wigged women and their children. Never the two together, the men and the women. Young males dressed old, burdened or given status by their uniform of difference. Is there some inherited ocular weakness? They don't see outsiders, invaders; they walk through, push us aside. Time is a value. There are no wanderers, no open agendas. I have witnessed the youths, coats off, scampering in Springfield Park on Sunday mornings, chasing footballs, but I had never, until this most recent expedition, seen an Orthodox man rambling up the east bank of the Lea, sprawled on a bench staring at water. 'A bench,' Yang Lian says, 'sinks deep into its own nature.'

The Chinese poet, now living on the crest of the hill above Abney Park cemetery, and beyond the Morrisons superstore, was born in Switzerland in 1955. He spent his childhood in

Beijing. In the 1970s, along with so many others from the academic and diplomatic classes, he was sent into the countryside. When he returned to the city, he joined the group of poets associated with the literary magazine *Jintian*. His poem *Norlang* was criticised by government agencies operating an 'Anti-Spiritual Pollution' programme. Lian was invited to give readings in Australia and New Zealand. After the Tiananmen protests, the savage state response, he chose to become a poet in exile, settling in London in 1997.

I watched Lian perform, giving interviews at conferences and literary festivals in Germany: he was intense, voluble, committed to his perceived destiny. Which he laid out in what New Labour would call a mission statement: 'Give me a single breath and I will grow roots, penetrate the soil, probe shingle and magma, and hear the sea through every artery and vein of groundwater, sharing the voyage of every navigator since the dawn of time.'

No modesty, false or otherwise, flouted here. Yang Lian was unashamed of his calling and his lineage. He saw the V of wild ducks in flight, crossing his Stamford Hill window, and took them for a welcome sign, a letter in his personal alphabet. He remained in one place long enough to number the season's last apples on a neighbour's tree. He spoke of a process of self-excavation, worrying at the water-margin he discovered on his doorstep, the deep metaphor that was Springfield Park. He relished the silence of this tributary street, its dark-coated ghosts like confirming elders of a previous existence in another country.

Stoke Newington has a way of absorbing exoticism, giving shelter, without fuss, to writers such as Joseph Conrad and Yang Lian. Toleration without celebration: the Chinese poet, with his spacious flat, his scrolls and bowls, books and bleached bird skulls, passed unnoticed. With his wife Yo Yo he operated a literary website – the 'snow-white' skeleton of a small bird was their icon. This fetish, retrieved from the marshes, reminded me of the Hebridean Steve Dilworth, the hierarchies of dead things waiting for his intricate caskets. Nature-sculptures found, not made; made to be found, then hidden away. Modest antidotes to the inflationary tendencies of public art. The compulsion to force the crowd to look up, not to notice the ground beneath their feet. The delicate snail shells on which they are about to trample.

YoYo poured the tea. Her husband, in the push of numerous projects, the excitement of publication, apologised for the curb he would have to put on our conversation. Discreetly, he watched the clock. He was discomforted by the fact that he had been too preoccupied, that morning, to wash. His hair was long, his eyes hot. He was fit for purpose and pumped to expound a story made from fixed elements, around which he circled, again and again. Taking breath, punctuating the monologue with excited emphasis, he struggled to bring a sentence to resolution. It wasn't, in truth, a conversation, but an audience with a privileged person. A poet. I placed the recorder on the table and off he went.

🐦

I have been travelling, all over the world, many times. It's not that I am everywhere, but everywhere is inside of me. This is true of Lea Valley. We base our individual discoveries on the idea that both the place and we ourselves are new, or renewed by the dialogue between place and ourselves. It is not a general Lea Valley but my *Lea Valley. Lea Valley is very special and different from other places.*

I myself am a valley, like my poem. Or like a river. The movement goes down. Every poet is an archaeologist of now. The layers of this time are within the moment of where we are. It's not cancelled time, but all time brought into one moment. I feel Lea Valley is a wonderful chance for me to see how deep the self, or selves, could be.

I did some research on this area. Lea Valley is part of London today, but it was once the border of Saxon and Viking kingdoms.

There was a Roman camp in Springfield Park. An ice age made this landscape. All of those realities are part of myself. All those layers make a dialogue of my memories, including other layers from other places. I write about other rivers: Hutuo, Hudson, Parramatta. All those rivers I have been to before. They become part of Lea Valley, within the river banks. Lea Valley is me. I am the Lea Valley.

I don't try to compare the Olympic experience in Beijing directly with what is happening in Lea Valley. But it's a general problem of the world, this commercial use of landscape. I witnessed the destruction of history in Beijing. History and classical Chinese culture have been totally covered over and destroyed by so-called globalisation, by ugly buildings. That is a new way to cut our memories, to root them out.

Lea Valley is being destroyed all the time. *It is always being destroyed: by old industries, football grounds. They transform everything. The authorities have tried their best to convert the marshland, the original view, to a more commercial use.*

As poets, we know that we have become important. Only by our deep experience, our studies, can we keep the soul of the landscape. We can remember the original creative power we gain from the land. I am now a British citizen, but, when my stranger's eyes look on Lea Valley, I recognise how rich are the links between the depths of the local and my experience of other places. I deeply hope the London Olympics are not only for commercial gain, but for the discovery of this other spirit. The invisible link between this land and mine.

The key word, not only for Lea Valley, but all other matters, is awareness. *Poetry is the best way to show understanding and awareness. Lea Valley must be a base of spirit, not only a base of sport. The government and the commercial bodies don't know that vision or have that understanding. They think of Lea Valley as a place of nothing. They don't have a vision of real development, the development of the mind. They only see more buildings. We, the poets, need to tell them, or at least to write down, that awareness is our poetry.*

When I walk in London, I love those so-called canals. They're beautiful. London is pretty low-lying, a lot of marshland. Chelsea was originally marshland. Now of course it has the most expensive buildings. Luckily, we have a small piece of marshland that has been left, here in Hackney. When I walk through these marshes it is hard to believe I am almost in the centre of London. It is both wild and alive. It reminds me of the wild geese, crying as they cross the sky. In Chinese characters the flying shape is exactly the character for 'human'. It is the sign or symbol for 'homesickness'.

In the Lea Valley context, this homesickness is not only for China, but for man. *For the original life of the land. Those wild geese remind me of this, otherwise I would be cut off. If we lose awareness, we can become so poor, so boring.*

London has always been a base for exchange between the very high culture of China and England. You tell me that Arthur Waley loved the River Lea? Lea Valley has a link with classical Chinese landscape. The water, the waves: it has a classical Chinese melancholy beauty. I'm totally not surprised by Waley's love for this place. The moon in the river. Huge clouds. I took many photographs. I could make a Lea Valley photo show with the poems. The skies are so dramatic.

So, to come back to where we start: human beings are always inspired by nature and the discovery of nature in themselves. You have a link between man and his discovery of nature and roots in locality. Then you find you have a link with all great classical poets in all languages: Goethe, Homer, Dante, Li Po, Du Fu. Everyone. *This is the key:* we translate everyone into ourselves.

If we think of the new Olympic structures in Lea Valley as being like Beijing, we should understand that in China the Games were run as a dictatorship toy. A part of the propaganda of Communism. The apparent links between the two Olympics are so shameful. It would be shameful for London to think that the Olympics would only be done for commercial reasons.

The only deep energy that happens inside these epochal cultural transformations, in China and in Britain too, is the poetry or the eyes of poetry. Then we could say, there is *a link, and a very great link.*

The landscape is inspiration, I think. The external landscape is an inspiration in front of our eyes. But, finally, poetry builds up the inner landscape, inside our hearts and minds. Inner knowledge also includes all the spiritual understanding in the idea of forms and in discovery of landscape. This is what brought the human soul to connect with the Olympics in Greece, originally. The transformation of external landscape into inner landscape, that is the power of spirit. I don't know how, but if somebody can see this point, then anything is possible.

❧

Lian's loved and recognised reed beds, the Walthamstow Marshes, beyond Springfield Park, acted as a mirror between his own flat, with its accumulation of memory objects, and the home, on the far side of the river, of one of his translators, Pascale Petit. They would meet and discuss the progress of the work in that borderland café. 'To Lian's eyes,' Petit said, 'the café walls are banded Mesozoic rock where Li Bai and Du Fu's shadows pass, each drunk on their own solitude.'

This is the loss we fear most: the contemplative solitude of the water margin, its accumulation of voices. Rivers and canals flow through us, changing and not changing, catching the rays of the rising sun and the transit of clouds. I came to Hackney by tracking the towpath out of Camden to the tempting expanse of Victoria Park. I made my compromises with the life of the place by establishing a way out, up the Lea Valley: which was scarred, hurt, inscribed along every inch of its urban-pastoral beauty. The Lea solaced Izaak Walton, Arthur Waley and, in our own time, the photographer Stephen Gill. The explanations of its power are always different. Whether it offers a willow-shaded fishing spot or edge-of-city grounds for wandering and cycling, the attraction lies in its accessible obscurity. The knowledge that nothing is explained or morally improving, overwhelmed by great public schemes.

Water is memory: repetition, erasure, inspiration. Without these canals, navigations, buried streams, the urban narrative thickens and chokes. If Springfield Park was lost, I would walk away. There are other rivers, other stories, in which, like Yang Lian, to search for the ghost of myself. Other, greater mountains of the mind. But here is the place, when conditioned reflexes close down, to which my feet still carry me.

On the Virtues of Dis-Enchantment

by Richard Mabey

'Very flat, Norfolk'. Noel Coward's put-down has become a standard reflex by outsiders to any suggestion that East Anglia is *real* landscape, stuck as it is between a fen and a wet place. And of course his quip wasn't just aimed at the seemingly bland topography, but at the inhabitants too, suggesting that we also are featureless, taciturn, dull, retarded. Webfeet, as we're still occasionally tagged. You will understand that we regard it as a slander, and an outlandish piece of geographical determinism. Anyone who still believes in regional characteristics, and that East Anglians are essentially suspicious, fatalistic, diffident, introverted, or any of the other clichés that are commonly banded about, needs to widen their circle of acquaintances.

But is there a partial truth buried in it? Does landscape influence mind-set? Shape peoples' responses to change? The doyen of East Anglian writers, Ronald Blythe, wonders whether 'landscape enters the blood with the milk.' Quite possibly, but what does it do there? Set the blood racing? Or clot it, making people not just prisoners but puppets of their native place? The two quintessential ingredients of the East Anglian landscape, wind and water, appear to have done both, not so much because of the region's flatness as its lowness. Much of it lies only a few metres above sea-level. It's been tilting down towards the North Sea for millennia. It *floats* on water – webs of underground springlines and tidal oozes that are forever on the point of reclaiming the surface. When the water joins forces with a wind that is howling in uninterrupted from the Caucasus, it can produce cataclysms like the 1953 tidal surge floods. 307 people lost their lives along the East Coast that January night, and 180,000 acres were lost to the sea. There are plaques marking the tidal high point inside the local pubs at Orford in Suffolk, and only non-East Anglians will be surprised to hear that some of the regulars held their ground, and sat drinking on the tables while the water lapped their seats.

If there isn't such a thing as a regional character, there is a shared narrative, an ongoing conversation about ourselves. Like all essentially rural people, East Anglians tell stories, pub stories, literary stories, tall stories. The narratives are cumulative. They become a kind of regional gossip, a communal self-portrait, a background hum that is part of the region's ambience. Sometimes they are dramatically acted out and become literal parts of the landscape.

And if there is a defining East Anglian narrative, a story that shapes the region's sense of its own identity, it is the parable of inundation. Flooding has always been part of the region's folk-memory, but rising sea-levels from global warming are now making it a regular part of most inhabitants' personal experience. Every couple of years, the sea breaches the coastal defences along the Norfolk coast at Cley and Salthouse. Houses at Happisburgh and Covehithe and Dunwich are simply falling into the waves, as the sea eats away at the cliffs. Even far inland, risk-taking housing developments on flood-plains are courting misery and massive insurance claims. The locals shake their heads at these new incursions: living where there is no barrier between you and the horizon means that housing, tourists, even modern life itself can take on the louring complexion of the Flood.

But the narrative is not a simple horror story. The long intimacy with water has generated a relationship that is more like enthralment than fear. If there has been an endless battle to keep the water out, there has also been a continuing compulsion to let it in – to the imagination and the heart. East Anglians are magicians with water. They eulogise it, paint it, conjure it into extraordinary forms. They treat it with the kind of respectful chutzpah that a snake charmer shows to a snake. When I lived on the north Norfolk coast in the 1970s, I discovered that my village, Blakeney, held a marshland sports day. It was a gauntlet thrown at the sea, a maritime fête for the reckless. There was a greasy pole quivering above the narrow channel of tidal water that runs past the quay. There was a marsh marathon, out to Blakeney Point and back over a mile of creeks and quaking mud – any combination of transport forms allowed. There were harrowing contests in dodgy boats.

One year, the closing event was a barrel relay-race over the channel, boys against girls, with no quarter given and no handicaps. It was an exhausting race. Each participant had to nudge a barrel across about ten yards of moving water, then swim back and start the next team member off. The tide was ebbing and the muddy edges of the channel were becoming slippery. The girls were beginning to struggle with the lolloping casks, which seemed to have minds of their own in the gathering tide-race. Then inspiration struck. They threw all the remaining barrels into the water, jumped in *en masse* after them, and ferried the whole lot over in one go, like a raft. The boys looked shocked, but seemed to decide that they didn't want to win the girls' way, and continued sullenly taking their barrels across one by one. But it was the girls who'd tapped into East Anglia's indigenous wisdom, which is pragmatic, canny, opportunist – what, in a boat, you'd describe as tacking. It is about accepting transience and capriciousness, and making the best of things. My late friend Roger Deakin made the ultimate local odyssey by *swimming* across Suffolk, through off-limits parkland lakes and weedy streams and the underwater maze of fugitive channel markers in the Blythe estuary, out to where Suffolk dissolves seamlessly into the sea. He called the book of his nationwide swimming adventure *Waterlog*.

It was a very local pun. East Anglian language is one of the markers of the region's sense of what it is. Although there is less rainfall here than anywhere else in Britain, there are more dialect words for water than the Inuit have for snow. They are vivid and evocative and always touched with a hint of self-mockery – essential if your home landscape lies on shifting sands. 'Dinge' is a grey drizzle. 'Grups' are the little drainage channels cut between a lane and a ditch. 'Claggy' is clotted with moisture.

I like to think that the indigenous landscape shares qualities with the language. It's legerdemain with the local stuff. Norfolk's flatness is really a sleight of hand, or perspective, only true from a landsman's earthbound standpoint. Take a more amphibious view, and the landscape appears as up and down as a corner of Cornwall. It's honeycombed with myriads of ingenious hollows and diggings and dykes that local people (and local nature) have made in order to get to grips with, make a profit from, or simply amuse themselves with water. Where I live now, in the Waveney Valley, the one-time fenland commons are riddled with little pools, the results of peat-digging on a cottage scale. There are moats, commoner in East Anglia than anywhere else: moats round houses, stackyards, parks, whole commons; moats as reservoirs, fences, fish-ponds, status symbols. There are thin channels dug exclusively for reed-cutters, and ephemeral treacle swamps where sugar-beet stands have been flash-flooded.

East Anglia's best-known water features, the Norfolk Broads, were created when medieval peat mines were flooded in the late middle ages. They – and their mother town, Great Yarmouth – are on the front-line of the new East Anglian floods, as sea changes threaten them from the east and human tides from the south and west.

They've responded in quite different ways. Yarmouth has always had the worst of it, pushed about by outsiders, always at the mercy of the rise and fall of the fishing. It began in a very East Anglian way, as a camp for migratory fishermen on a growing band of sand and silt across the mouth of the River Yare. The bank, as one medieval writer put it, 'waxed in height and greatness'. The herring catch waxed too, and Yarmouth grew into a prosperous fishing and trading port, the foremost shipping town in Britain at one time. Tourism discovered it in about 1750 and, before the end of the century, the first theatres and bowling greens had arrived on the front. Two Yarmouths developed – the fun-town out on the sea's edge, the Golden Mile; and the working port about half a mile inland, clustered around the long harbour formed by the confluence of the rivers Yare, Bure and Waveney.

Both were bombed to smithereens in World Wars I and II, and what was left of the old port was bulldozed away during the 1960s. Twenty years later the herrings – the immemorial 'silver harvest' – were gone too, fished out by industrial trawlers. Yarmouth has begun to remake itself as a deepwater container port, and there are spreading new suburbs. But it still feels like a hurt and dislocated community, under a kind of foreign occupation. Down by the new harbour you can see the jobless and the memory-haunted, gazing out at the huge computer-operated ships, and listening in to their chatter on short-wave radios.

Yarmouth was from the start a gateway to the Norfolk Broads. The old diggings – largely run by the big local monasteries – were flooded by an increase in high tides and rainfall in the 13th century. For the best part of 600 years, Broadland was a self-contained culture, 400 square miles of open water and marsh, a subsistence economy of rough grazing, duck-hunting, eel-fishing, reed-cutting and peat-digging, the likes of which would have been hard to find this side of the Danube Delta. Leisure boating didn't become popular until the 1880s. It was the making and, for a few decades, the breaking of the place. From the 1960s to the '90s, boat effluent combined with chemical run-off from neighbouring agricultural land began to poison the watercourses. Vegetation and fish died off. What had been an ecological paradise came close to turning into the aquatic equivalent of a run-down housing estate.

But the Broads were rescued. A raft of measures from speed limits for motor-cruisers to dredging weed-choked navigation channels has begun to restore the vitality of the place. As the price of fuel rises, so more sailing craft move in. The whole area is now a National Park, and one of the richest wildlife areas in lowland Britain. Though there are new developments around the bigger Broadland villages, the place never feels colonised, as Yarmouth does. And the home-grown contribution to the housing stock lifts the heart with its refusal to play by Barrett and Bovis rules. Along the banks of the Yare and its dykes in Potter Heigham there's an extraordinary (and still growing) settlement of vernacular buildings. Many were self-builds in the early years of the 20th century, clapboard cabins put up as fishing shacks or weekend boating huts. They evolved, as often as not, into family holiday retreats and occasionally into retirement dwellings – becoming models, without ever being planned in that way, for the fashionable idea of 'flexible housing'. They've been customised with tremendous elan, with all east Anglia's native wit. There are miniature windmills, thatched bungalows, riverfront gardens done up with statues of Andy Kapp and Rupert Bear and the Greek goddess Ceres. Many, in this place that has always conjured with wind as well as water, are buckling on wind generators. In summer even the ice cream man arrives by boat.

All this may be undone, the scientists say, by global warming. The freshwater Broads will be drowned by seawater, the gentle rivers become aggressively tidal, the kingfishers vanish, and Rupert Bear will be sunk up to his scarf. In the medium term, there's not much doubt that some of this will happen. The sea is chipping away at the coastal defences all round the coast. The idea that they can be endlessly repaired and raised to keep pace with the rising sea-level has already been officially abandoned. Such a policy would bankrupt any low-lying country. Even Holland, whose precocious understanding of the sea's incursions helped drain East Anglia in the 17th century, has given up attempting to repel the sea at any cost. On both sides of the North Sea the new policy is 'managed retreat'. The big and important settlements will be defended, but elsewhere the sea will find its way in eventually and be allowed to form new saltmarsh, the best and most natural buffer to the tides. In the Broads, fresh-water, fen, people and wildlife will all have to move further inland, and higher up the valley sides, which will mean a new kind of habitat creation – a barrel-lumping move, something entirely within the scope of the indigenous imagination. It was flooding, after all, that created the Broads in the first place.

Water adds both detail and indefiniteness to a landscape. If East Anglia's flatness is an illusion in the vertical dimension, it is also horizontally. The Broadland marshes, the Waveney valley fens, the north Norfolk saltings – they are all electric with subtle and shifting particularities. The cord-grass bounces in the returning tide, the butterfly weaves between the sails, the still water ripples. And then, in a matter of an hour, or a day, it is all transformed. The wind gets up, the waters rise. You look out at a field in the evening and in the morning it is lake, the old adversary reclaiming ground it occupied half a millennium ago. Perhaps it is this mercurial quality that generates such a reverence for the luminous detail of things and places, as if in a landscape that is both spare and transient, every shard and nugget counts. East Anglia nourishes clear, unabstract responses.

The poet Edward Thomas, beachcombing at Minsmere on the Suffolk coast before he went off to be killed in Arras trenches, made a collection as telling as the Sutton Hoo treasure: 'champagne corks, sailor's hats, Antwerp beer bottles, fish boxes, oranges, lemons, onions, banana stems, waterworn timber and the most exquisite flat and round pebbles, black, white, dove grey, veined, wheat coloured. Why does nature make these beautiful things so carelessly and then one wonders whether all beautiful objects are not of this careless inevitableness.' The sea brings back what it takes away. Water changes things, but everywhere makes renewal a continuous possibility.

My second eastern bolthole after Blakeney was a cottage on the edge of the grazing marshes of the Blythe valley, just west of Blythburgh itself, and in sight of that famously airy church where Cromwell's lads had fun shooting up the carved angels in the roof. On my first night there I lay awake listening to nightingales, singing with that beautiful and careless inevitableness. One was on the little heath above the house, the other in the churchyard of Wenhaston St Peter, where there is a riotous 16th-century screen-painting of the Last Judgement. Nikolaus Pevsner, not understanding what East Anglia was about at all, described it as 'distressingly rustic'.

Now I've settled permanently in Norfolk. I'd got into a rut in my homeland in the Chilterns, fallen ill, and drifted by a strange combination of serendipity and logic (a classic East Anglian cocktail) towards what I'd always thought of as my second home. It was the sense of possibility that set me right. The floods that autumn were like a second spring, quickening the place, pulling strings, jerking earth and vegetation – and me – back into life.

The house lies on the edge of what's known as the Breckland, a huge bowl of sandy soils at the very centre of East Anglia. The name comes from the Old English word *brek*, meaning a tract of land that was broken up for cultivation and then abandoned for up to twenty years to allow it to regain its fertility. It was the only kind of primitive agriculture that was sustainable on these thin soils. By the 18th century, it had become 'a vast Arabian desert', a place of sand-blown sheep-walks and rabbit warrens. There was an inland lighthouse near Brandon to guide benighted travellers.

Even here there was inundation. In 1688 the village of Santon Downham was buried by a sandstorm. It rose again in the early years of the 20th century as the local headquarters of the Forestry Commission.

Breckland's recent history as a convenient place to dump conifer plantations and military bases has been similar to that of many areas conventionally regarded as 'wasteland'. Much of the rest of the old prairieland has been tamed, and grows geese and asparagus and carrots on an industrial scale. There are vast stud farms, done up like South Fork, with neo-classical porticos and security fencing to match the US air-bases'. Many of the ancient trackways across the Brecks, including England's oldest road, the Icknield Way, have been stopped off at the edge of the big shooting estates. Modern Breckland feels, as new Yarmouth does, as if it has been taken out of East Anglia, expropriated. It was named for its canny local adaptation to transience, but is now the most impenetrable and enclosed part of the whole region.

In the extreme north-west Breckland merges with the Fens, which stretch into Cambridgeshire and Lincolnshire. This is where the East Anglian narrative does become stereotyped. Locals living outside the Fens have an inexhaustible supply of slanderous stories about the inhabitants of this drained swamp, inland from the Wash. They are, the myths go, insular, inbred, violent, mad. They're where the doctor's shorthand NFN – 'normal for Norfolk' – comes into its own. The Fens are Eastern England's Balkans, the butt of all malicious jokes.

There has been some substance in these images. Isolation, minimal public services, a physical environment bleaker than anywhere in England and the corrosive effects of half a century of intensive chemical farming have left their mark. In the 19th century 'the ague' and malaria were endemic, and opium use was widespread until the 1920s. In the 1960s and '70s depression was common, and 'fen syndrome', described as a kind of 'cultural retardation', was a recognised medical condition.

Things are improving. Young Poles and Portuguese pick the vegetables now. But like all gang-workers, they're paid a pittance and live in minimal comfort, and it's doubtful if intensive agriculture is socially and ecologically sustainable much longer in many parts of the Fens. Already an alternative land use is surfacing. Across the whole area East Anglia's love-hate relationship with inundation is moving into a love phase. From Whittlesey Mere in the west to Lakenheath in the east, half a dozen major projects are restoring the landscape to true fen, the mix of open water, reedbed, wet woodland and grazing marsh that it was before the days of large-scale drainage. Conservation bodies such as the National Trust and the Royal Society for the Protection of Birds are making the running, and there are already some 30,000 hectares earmarked for restoration.

But this isn't a grand exercise in human abandonment. All the bodies are working closely with Fenland villages and sympathetic local farmers, and the end result should be a diverse and regenerated human landscape as well as a vast wildlife reserve, with hardy cattle grazing the wetlands, and small-scale industry based around indigenous resources like reed and willow. There might even be some new village Amsterdams on the edge of the restored watercourses, architect-designed versions of the Broadland shanty settlements.

For the past century or so the Fens have confirmed to Noel Coward's dismissive image. They were not just flat but flattened. If the new projects work they may restore the area to an earlier East Anglian image of itself, as a place where people go with the flow.

'MOSS GREEN', SEVENOAKS, KENT

May Morn

by Jane Rendell

Note: The captions to the eight photographs that follow are taken from a text, originally entitled 'Moss Green', written as one in a series of three, contained within a critical essay on the work of artist Elina Brotherus and published as 'Longing for the Lightness of Spring'.[1]

The house is beautiful – a one-storey building, with a square plan – born at the birth of modernism in the aftermath of the First World War.

It embodies the values of early English modernism, of the Arts and Crafts movement: 'truth to materials' and honest craftsmanship.

From the road it looks a little unloved, in need of some care and attention. Up close it is clearly derelict, almost in ruins.

We enter a room with windows at each end. Curtains are falling away from the runners.

The fabric has been soaked overnight and is drying in the spring afternoon sunshine.

On the window sill and spilling over onto the floor are piles of old magazines. The pages are stuck together and disintegrate if you try to pull them apart.

There are some photographs of buildings. One is particularly damp; the corners are soft, the surface is wrinkled.

It shows a tower block, just completed, empty and pristine, a moss green utopia, the modernist dream dispersing as it soaks up spring rain.

In 2001 curator Jules Wright from the Wapping Project in London invited me to write an essay about artist Elina Brotherus's work *Spring*. It was composed of two installations: a video triptych, *Rain, The Oak Forest, Flood* (2001) in the boiler house, and a back-lit image, *Untitled* (2001), measuring three metres by eight metres and reflected in the water tank on the roof of the Wapping Project. *Untitled* showed an illuminated horizon dividing sky from earth: the pale grey sky of Iceland floating above what was once viscous lava now covered in green moss.

Rain, The Oak Forest and *Flood* were projected on screens hung from the ceiling. In the first video, the viewer, located on the inside of a window, watched, as rain streamed down the outside of the glass. The second showed an oak forest after the rain had stopped, but when drops, still heavy, continued to fall to the ground, John Betjeman's 'second rain'. The third video was of a flood: a forest of elegant trees rose silver from a pane of shining water.

In responding to *Spring*, I found myself returning to scenes – real and imagined, remembered and dreamed – that corresponded with Brotherus' images and supplemented her landscapes with places of my own. The three places I described made spatial, material and visual associations with Brotherus' *Spring*. In 'Moss Green', I remembered a derelict house in the green belt where in spring we found photographs of a brave new world of modernist high-rise housing. Just after the autumn equinox, just after her death, I dreamt of the shrouded home of my Welsh great aunt. 'White Linen' recalled the presence of life in the form of plants in this dream, while 'Bittersweet' recounted another spring visit, this time to an abandoned cork factory in Catalunya, where we found the names of the colours scattered, abandoned, all over the floor: black, white, orange, turquoise, bittersweet.

Anticipating the end of winter, *Spring* opened in Wapping just after the autumn equinox in the northern hemisphere. Curatorially, the work faced towards the long decline into winter, the season from which it desired to turn away. Paralleling this juxtaposition which poised spring's hope for winter's retreat right at its early edge, I positioned *Spring*'s foregrounding of anticipation as a yearning that looks forward to new life, against my own fascination with the backwards gaze of nostalgia. My three texts connected Brotherus' landscapes, infused with anticipatory longing, to places tinted by nostalgia, constructing a tension between life and death, rejuvenation and decay, a looking forward and a turning backward.

❕

My first visit to the house I came to call 'Moss Green' had occurred in the spring of 2001. For the next decade I was to walk past it several times a year, as part of my weekly Sunday walk. Every Sunday morning, whatever the weather, taking a flask of hot soup to be supped under the dripping branches of winter trees, or a picnic to be eaten in a sunlit meadow, my partner and I make the journey to Waterloo or London Bridge, and board a train taking us to the limit of the metropolis – to London's so-called green belt. After an about an hour (and, more recently, with the collapse of the Sunday rail network, more like two) we disembark the train and walk into the dusk along the paths of the Weald.

In our walks out of Sevenoaks we sometimes take the route down Oak Lane, then Grassy Lane, past Fig Street, and then along Gracious Lane, drawing to a halt at the fork in the road where Moss Green is situated. When we first saw the house we were entirely enchanted, with the way of life it represented as well as the arresting beauty of its slow yet gentle decay. The house was single storey, of a brick and timber construction, placed at the top of a scarp slope – with its porch looking out over southern England, under which two benches faced one another. The interior was full of exquisite touches: a perfectly placed built-in cupboard, a carefully detailed window sill and frame, a thoughtful light switch, a door handle that fitted like a glove. It was hovering at that point where the decay was still able to provide an atmosphere of charm, where the thought of collapse could be held off, and where it was still possible to imagine oneself into the house, repairing the woodwork and occupying the rooms. We guessed it had probably been built after the First World War, perhaps as part of the programme – 'Homes fit for Heroes' – which allowed returning and often traumatized soldiers to readjust to civilian life in the comfort of a simple domestic setting with space for gardening and growing food.

But over the years the house has increasingly fallen into disrepair, and our spirits now sink each time we see it. When its slate roof was removed around three years ago the rot really set in and as a structure it is now barely stable. As it slipped passed the threshold of being 'save-able'; we have surrendered our dream of living there ourselves in a modest rural retreat. No doubt the new owner is waiting for the moment of collapse, when the walls cave in, in order to construct a dwelling which requires no restorative work. I wonder whether Moss Green should have been listed, whether I should have taken on that task myself. And if it is not valued as a piece of architectural heritage, what are those emotional qualities it holds that make it feel special enough to want to save?

On one visit, years ago, when the house was open to the elements, but some of its contents still present, we noted books on architecture, old journals from the building trade, and piles of photographs. We salvaged a few items – notably one book, *New Architecture of London: A Selection of Buildings since 1930*,[2] along with a selection of back and white photographs, some of which are reproduced here.

Recently, in examining the photographs more closely, I have become fascinated with tracking down the buildings imaged in them. As well as the architectural qualities of the structures, I have had five text-based clues to work with – a board in front of one block of flats with the name: 'Ernest Knifton Ltd.'; a car parked outside another with the registration plate SLX 956; a street sign reading 'Westmoreland Terrace'; and letters over the entrances to two other buildings with the words '1–24 Edmund Street' and 'Witl-'.

In working between *New Architecture of London* as well as web searches for the various clues, I have managed to track down most of the structures. It turns out that the majority are what we now regard as modernist icons, such as Elmington Estate (1957), Picton Street, London SE5, designed by the LCC Architect's Dept., now largely demolished; Hallfield Estate (1952–55), Bishops Bridge Road, W2, designed by Tecton, Drake and Lasdun for Paddington Borough Council; Alton East Estate (1952–55), Portsmouth Road, SW15, designed by the LCC Architect's Dept.; Alton West Estate (1955–59), Roehampton Lane, SW15, designed by the LCC Architect's Dept. and Churchill Gardens (1950–62), Grosvenor Road, Lupus Street, SW1, designed by Powell and Moya for Westminster City Council.

At the same time I have been searching for a new flat of my own in London to live in. Having just sold a home on the eleventh floor of a 1950s block designed by Joseph Emberton, I am looking for a place to buy and to live in that matches it in terms of design quality, space standards and view. So I took the opportunity to view these buildings via primelocation.com. The search revealed their 'value' in economic terms, as property, as commodities with prices. From an estate agent's perspective, these flats are described as ideal investments, not as places where the purchaser might choose to live, but rather as buy-to-let opportunities, real estate to be rented out to students and others. The images of fully occupied domestic settings on the property website provided an interesting counterbalance to the just completed exteriors photographed from the outside, positioning the architecture as a commodity to be purchased by individuals as well as (or instead of?) social entities to be lived in by communities.

Searching for modernist icons through primelocation.com has been a stark reminder of what has happened to the socialist ideals of modernism. Some of the modern movement's public housing projects have become oases of cool property in the London postcodes associated with the rich. Those in the west of the capital have often been well maintained and sometimes privatised and provided with concierge schemes, and others in areas of regeneration have been connected with the aspirations of up and coming neighbourhoods and the somewhat grimy conditions of their rather neglected public spaces – lifts, stairways and façades – overlooked by purchasers keen to be part of the lifestyles offered by certain parts of London in terms of cultural cachet: independent boutiques, cafés and galleries.

Those pieces of modern architecture in the poorer boroughs, outside the pockets of existing wealth, and the aspiring regeneration zones, have been allowed to decline materially, often not included in 'major works' programmes – the large-scale council repair and maintenance cycles. Often located in so-called 'sink estates', many of the blocks house the poorest families in London. Some have been demolished either because the years of neglect have led to conditions of terminal dereliction, or because the original construction is viewed to be too expensive to overhaul. But the seeming pragmatic solution offered by viewing the problems through economic concerns, is a symptom, or perhaps a problem of perception. Modern architecture is often seen as intimately tied to social deprivation and this has forced the designers of certain regeneration schemes to adopt a new architectural language: one which is not so obviously 'modern' and is therefore capable of suggesting optimism, community and better standards of living in a different way.

But what of the person who lived in Moss Green and once owned the photographs of these modern buildings? Was he or she an architect, and if so did they play a role in designing the buildings in the photographs? How did they compare these schemes for urban mass housing with their own rural bungalow. If the delicate beauty of Moss Green points outwards to a whole network of modernist icons, how should one compare these two modernisms – the earlier vernacular craft-based phase of the Arts and Crafts with the later phase of industrialisation and standardization?

From Tacita Dean's work, critiquing the heroism of modernism by pointing to the failure of certain technological schemes, such as *Delft Hydraulics* (1996) or *Sound Mirrors* (1999), to Rut Blees Luxemburg's glowing photographs of north London's high-rise flats, entitled *Caliban Towers I and II*, from *London – A Modern Project* (1997), which titles modernist architecture as a monster, there has been a recent fascination with the so-called failure of the modern project. In some cases, this takes the form of a wistful melancholy for modernism's passing, at other times a more gleeful delight at the collapse of a social dream, that some see as too forceful and others as ridiculously idealistic.[3]

But I'm not so sure modernism has failed. Rather, I think the aspirations for social community and progress it embodies have been driven out, in England at least, by a Conservative and then a Labour government keen to promote an ideology of home-ownership. If everyone is weighed down by a hefty mortgage, the capacity for dissent is drastically reduced. Losing a day's pay by striking might easily mean loosing the roof over one's head. There is a lot at stake when the social housing of the modernist project is sold off as 'a good opportunity for investment' on primelocation.com; it is perhaps not overstating the case to suggest it has created a disaster for the left, not only because the number of homes available to let by the council are reduced for those who need them, but also because those who buy them become part of the propertied class and all that entails. I know this because I am part of the problem. There is no doubt that I would have remained closer to the truth of my political ideals if I had continued to rent a room, as I did in my student days. Friends who live in other European cities, in Barcelona and Berlin for example, still do just that.

But am I really as monstrous as an investor who purchases a flat in a modernist icon to leverage out an income in rent. Does it make a difference that I still aspire to dwell within the modernist ideal, that my home is not simply a commodity, that I enjoy living in a diverse community? The enchantment the high-rise holds for me is a blend of the aesthetic preferences my architectural education instilled in me, and my social ideals. And Jane Bennett's project inspires me – she breathes enchantment back into modernity – arguing against its status as a site of alienation.[4] Her writing makes me understand from a theoretical perspective how it might still be possible to view architecture's inhabitation of modernity with wonder.

In 1993 artist Alison Marchant made a work, *Field Study 3: Charged Atmospheres*, where she reproduced photographs dating back to the 1970s, thrown away from the National Monuments Records, blown up to life size. The decaying photographs showed neglected interiors, high ceilinged salons from London's Georgian building stock. The work doubled the materiality of decay and the related affects or emotional states associated with neglect and abandonment. The deterioration in *Charged Atmospheres* operates at the level of both signified and signifier – *abandoned* interiors appear in *abandoned* photographs.

The situation in my image-text work shown here is somewhat different; the material decay of the photographs, as ink and paper documents, is counteracted by the aspiration of the just-completed buildings in the images. In these photographs, the buildings – the signifieds – are new – they look ahead. It is only the photographs themselves – the signifiers – that bear the passage of time. The buildings are well attended to. Indeed, it might be that what holds them together is their place as the centre of attention in a tour of newly completed social housing projects – witness the group of men in overcoats pointing towards certain features. It is only the photographs themselves that have been left behind, to weather the rain on the Weald coming in through the open window over the years.

I have titled this image-text work *May Morn*.

Returning to Moss Green, once again, several weekends ago, much of the timberwork had collapsed and was lying in pieces over the grass. I turned one rotten section over to reveal two words, painted in fast fragmenting white letters, 'May Morn'. This, I remembered, was the building's name plaque, which had been located at the entrance to the plot, framed by brambles, when we first came across the house.

Morn and mourn are homonyms, one suggests a beginning, the other an ending. Morning begins the day, while mourning – in grieving the loss of something or someone – marks an ending. Due to their deteriorating material states, the Moss Green house, the paper of the photographs and the painted letters 'May Morn' all point towards their own disintegration, or endings; and yet the buildings contained within the photographs are shown at the beginning of their life. What does it mean, now, to turn back and examine these icons of modernism at an early moment – a spring-time – when hope for a better future was not viewed as a naïvely misjudged optimism.

On a bright spring day, a May morn no less, days before a general election, I remain hopeful, facing forward. This is not a time for mourning, not a time for grieving the failure of the modernist project: such a gesture needs to be resisted. The ideals of modernism are to be cherished, not only aesthetically but also, and importantly, politically. It is, I think, precisely *because* an aspiration for social change remains that we are being presented, continuously, with an image of modernism as a project that has collapsed. This is the myth-making of Capitalist ideology.

Writing positively of nostalgia, as a longing for something better, contemporary cultural critic Frederic Jameson has pointed out, with reference to the earlier work of Walter Benjamin on allegory and ruin, that looking back to a past because it appears to be better than the problems of the present is not necessarily regressive, especially if it can be used to change the future. He writes: 'But if nostalgia as a political motivation is most frequently associated with Fascism, there is no reason why a nostalgia conscious of itself, a lucid and remorseless dissatisfaction with the present on the grounds of some remembered plenitude, cannot furnish as adequate a revolutionary stimulus as any other...'.[5]

1. This essay was commissioned by Jules Wright of the Wapping Project, London and originally published as Jane Rendell, 'Longing for the Lightness of Spring', *Elina Brotherus* (London: The Wapping Project, 2001), pp. 19–26. This essay is part of my larger project of site-writing, initiated as a pedagogic tool at the Bartlett School of Architecture, UCL, from 2001, and as a mode of spatialising writing first in Jane Rendell, 'Doing it, (Un)Doing it, (Over)Doing it Yourself: Rhetorics of Architectural Abuse', Jonathan Hill (ed.), *Occupying Architecture* (London: Routledge, 1998), pp. 229–46, and then developed through a whole series of essays and works, brought together in Jane Rendell, *Site-Writing: The Architecture of Art Criticism* (London: I.B. Tauris, 2010).
2. Sam Lambert (ed.), *New Architecture of London: A Selection of Buildings since 1930* (London: The British Travel and Holidays Association in collaboration with the Architectural Association, 1963).
3. For a longer discussion of this point see Jane Rendell, *Art and Architecture: A Place Between* (London: I.B. Tauris, 2006).
4. See Jane Bennett, *The Enchantment of Modern Life: Attachments, Crossings and Ethics* (Princeton and Oxford: Princeton University Press, 2001).
5. Fredric Jameson, *Marxism and Form: Twentieth-Century Dialectical Theories of Literature* (Princeton: Princeton University Press, 1971), p. 82.

East of Eden

by Ken Worpole

I *People Without Names*

Just inside the churchyard gate of St Edmund King and Martyr, East Mersea, was a fresh burial mound, marked by a small hand-made wooden cross bearing the words, 'Unknown Person'. On first sight this tree-shaded village church, painted by Rex Whistler during a respite from military training in June 1940, seems to exemplify English pastoralism, yet it is only a single field away from the North Sea, where it meets the windswept estuary of the River Blackwater. St Edmund's was ministered by the Reverend Sabine Baring Gould between 1870 and 1881, though he is better known as the author of the stirring hymns, *Onward Christian Soldiers* and *Now The Day Is Over*, and of the marshland gothic novel, *Mehalah*: a man with so many children he could not remember their names.

The West Tower of St Edmund's served as a lookout point and beacon during times of war, and the beaches, seawalls and fields all along this coast remain punctuated by concrete pillboxes and fortified gun-emplacements, many now covered with graffiti and moss. Some are disappearing beneath the sand as shore levels rise, as they do on the shingle spit leading to Mersea Stone. Others have been pulverised to ruins by the sea. If these coastal fringes now often seem lonely and bereft of human activity, once no fewer than 300,000 men were deployed here during the first winter of the First World War building coastal defences, adopting the concrete bunker prototype from the Germans on the Western Front.[1] Such concrete outcrops are now as much a part of the Essex landscape as hay-barns, feed hoppers and milking sheds. During the same war some 2,000 people lived and worked on tiny Osea Island in the River Blackwater, building motor torpedo boats.[2] Today the island is home to a private health sanctuary and a handful of other residents, who plan their daily outings by the tides. The disappearance of a once thriving traffic of boats, transporting goods along the navigable rivers and coast, has left the Essex shoreline largely deserted.

Mersea Island has few claims to fame, though in 2006 the *Times Literary Supplement* reported that an American academic, Paul Streitz, arrived in Cambridge to give a lecture on the 17th Earl of Oxford and Elizabethan culture, during which he claimed that in 1604 Shakespeare 'was exiled to the island of Mersea in the English Channel', where he completed *The Tempest*. It would be a lovely story to believe; even so, for me the island is haunted in other ways. The dusty back lanes of high summer evoke powerful childhood memories of caravan holidays spent there, along with the self-punishing pleasures of swimming in the choppy sea, whose buoyancy made swimming seem like riding a carousel, while being repeatedly slapped in the face by draughts of salty water.

There are several inhabited islands off the Essex shoreline apart from Mersea, in addition to around thirty uninhabited ones. The latter number is as imprecise as the changing fractal mathematics of coastal landforms. Mersea itself is connected to the mainland by a permanent causeway known as the Strood. During high spring and autumn tides the island can be cut off from the mainland as the powerful estuary waters rush inland, covering the causeway road and filling the surrounding creeks, inlets and marshlands so that the whole area resembles, even briefly, a stretch of open sea. When the tide abates the island roads are covered in seaweed and driftwood. A distinctive feature of this coastal fringe of Essex is that, in the words of ecologist David Corke, 'the most extensive and important habitats spend half the time under the sea.'[3]

I came across the grave at St Edmund's during an early morning cycle ride several years ago, one of many I've made in this part of Essex. These forays started when my family first rented a caravan at Mill Beach on the Blackwater for a week's holiday in the late 1950s. The caravan site, with its 'pleasure beach' of shingle, concrete rubble and black mud, faced across the river to Northey Island where, in 991, a Viking army, under the command of the king of Denmark, disembarked from their fleet of longships and camped overnight before defeating the army of Byrhtnoth in a ferocious battle, not only presaging the end of Anglo-Saxon England but also producing that great, if incomplete, narrative poem, *The Battle of Maldon*. It is a flat landscape with water lying in many directions, and flat landscapes are, to my mind even more psychologically challenging than mountainous terrain. It is not a case of 'because it is there' but 'because you are here'. Ostensibly serene and untroubled, the Essex marshlands are also possessed of a distinctive melancholy, especially so in the winter months, which can either be character-forming or near-fatal.

Anonymous graves such as the one in St Edmund's churchyard are rare, and when found in coastal cemeteries usually indicate the burial of someone drowned at sea, whose body has been washed up unidentified. The *Friedhof der Namenlosen* in Vienna, the cemetery of the nameless, is devoted to those pulled dead from the Danube. There is a long tradition of respect and care afforded to such anonymous victims by maritime or riparian communities, which Larraine Worpole and I explored in the book, *Last Landscapes*, a series of essays and photographs exploring the relationship between death and landscape. For me, certainly, topography and mortality are interwoven, though I would not go as far as W.G. Sebald, who saw the whole world as one vast cemetery. Yet Sebald is not alone in his obsession with the *communita dei defunti*, given how many recent novels – for example John Berger's *Here Is Where We Meet*, Hilary Mantel's *Beyond*

Black, and Will Self's *How the Dead Live* – engage with the idea that the dead are always with us, as familiars and companions.

It is difficult to imagine these near-empty landscapes, occasionally punctuated by small settlements, as humanly bearable without the solace afforded by their churches, whether as beacons in the landscape or as quiet interiors. From Mersea Island one looks across the Blackwater estuary to the isolated Chapel of St Peter's, built by St Cedd of Lindisfarne in 654 AD and standing foursquare on the headland, a place of pilgrimage and retreat for more than a thousand years. Looking across the northern estuary of the River Colne, at the confluence of the Blackwater and the Colne, lies Brightlingsea where, in the churchyard of the larger and more prominent All Saints is the headstone and cenotaph of the Barber family:

IN LOVING MEMORY

CHARLES BARBER
AGED 46 YEARS
AND OF HIS SONS
THEODORE AND WALTER
AGED RESPECTIVELY 16 AND 14
WHO PERISHED WITH HIM AT SEA
SEPTEMBER 3rd 1884
ALSO OF HIS ELDEST SON
AGED 23 YEARS
WHO WAS DROWNED IN THE NORTH SEA
MARCH 6th 1883
ALSO OF
AGATHA CAPON BARBER
WIFE OF THE ABOVE
WHO DIED OCTOBER 5th 1920
AGED 84 YEARS

One's feelings here are not with the dead but the long-widowed and child-bereft survivor. The sea brings life and death, prosperity and terror. It also brings trade, and here the history changes. Travelling out to Essex from London one moves from the vast docks and warehouses of the Pool of London, thick in the 1950s with ships' funnels and tugboats (which I recall from accompanying my father during school holidays when he collected timber from the docks) to Ford's at Dagenham, in Essex proper, just a few miles downriver. Here one of the largest car factories in the world once operated with over 40,000 workers. Not any more. The seawall footpath then continues on to the factories and container yards of Tilbury, the oil refineries at Corringham, then further round the coast to the sequestered military lands of Foulness and Fingringhoe, passing boatyards, fishing ports and marinas. This Essex coastline embodies a melange of the maritime and the industrial, the defensive and the arcadian, much of it now redundant, and gaining a disputed etymology of its own: slack nature, post-industrial wilderness, unofficial countryside, working wild, drosscape, edge condition, *terrain vague*. It is this potent mixture of economy and geography that confounds and dismays contemporary landscape aesthetics.

Debates about landscape aesthetics are now gaining urgency, even if the UK's endorsement of the European Landscape Convention (Florence 2000) in 2006 caused scarcely a ripple in the political press. Article 5 states that, 'each party undertakes to recognise landscapes in law as an essential component of people's surroundings, an expression of the diversity of their shared cultural and natural heritage, and a foundation of their identity.' This growing appreciation of the importance of place now goes to the heart of politics and to issues of popular aesthetics and cultural identity. Yet consensus is hard to find on what is valued and what remains unloved. A survey of the landscape qualities of the English counties, which the magazine *Country Life* published in 2004, awarded Essex no marks at all for landscape quality, a judgement unsurprisingly resisted by those who live there.

If one is charitable, one might say that *Country Life*'s editors lacked imagination. They also failed to notice that the 20th century had been and gone, leaving considerable aesthetic confusion in its wake. Nearly a hundred years ago Thomas Hardy predicted, in connection with his description of the gloomy Egdon Heath, that 'one day people would go for harsher surroundings when looking for beauty: in Iceland rather than the vineyards of southern Europe, on the beaches of Scheveningen rather than in the spa towns of Baden or Heidelberg.'[4] Before him the painter John Constable wrote that 'I never saw an ugly thing in my life,' going on to record that 'the sound of water escaping from mill-dams, willows, old rotten planks, slimy posts, and brickwork, I love such things. These scenes made me a painter, and I am grateful.'[5]

There is now an urgent need to interpret and value contemporary landscapes anew, especially those that resist traditional categories of taste and approbation. The discussion of landscape aesthetics offers an arena in which social and environmental imperatives have the potential to be reconciled in a new kind of politics of place in the 21st century. However, it is an arena in which there are no easy compromises for those engaged in public policy, especially for those of us torn between conservation and innovation, along with residual hopes of radical future change. The 19th century French writer and provincial politician, Jules Reynard, wrote that 'as a mayor, I am responsible for the upkeep of rural roads. As a poet I would prefer to see them neglected.'[6] Similar ambivalences afflict us all, and the ability to live in uncertainties, and to accept contradictions, is certainly a requirement of modern life and letters.

II *Landscape with Figures?*

Where do the aesthetic conventions by which we judge landscape come from? The first artistic representations of landscape in Western culture arrived in the form of miniatures:

exquisitely painted illuminations found in early medieval Books of Hours. In his history of landscape art Kenneth Clarke wrote of how the 'illumination' fused both subject matter, the love of God, and an emotional mood through a suffusion of painted light, observing that 'it is no accident that this sense of saturating light grew out of a school of manuscript illuminations, and first appears in miniatures. For in such small images a unity of tone is more easily achieved, and the whole scene can be given the concentrated brilliance of reflection in a crystal.'[7] The quality of light and what that light suggests in the way of divination or immanent meaning still haunts contemporary landscape painting and photography.

As religious paintings took on a larger canvas, more detailed landscapes emerged, often painstakingly painted as backdrops to the great Biblical stories. Intriguingly these landscapes often reflected the painter's homeland topography, thus producing the paradox that many of the seminal events in both Old and New Testaments, presumed to have taken place in the 'Biblical lands' of the Middle East, ended up with Dutch or Italian settings as *mise-en-scène*. Thus, to take some of the most famous examples, Robert Campin's *The Nativity* (c.1425) foregrounds the Bethlehem stable against a verdant, meandering river valley, lined with a terrace of steep-roofed brick houses, Konrad Witz's *The Miraculous Draught of Fishes* (1444) is set against the shores of the lake of Geneva, the *Crucifixion* (c.1460) painted by Antonello da Messina 'with its dark sea and mountainous, irregular coast, clearly represents his native Sicily', and Patenier's richly coloured *Rest in the Flight into Egypt* (c.1520) has a deeply wooded background, high-gabled Dutch farmhouses, and Dutch peasants cutting golden fields of corn behind the Virgin and Child.[8]

Not that this was regarded as anachronistic. This cultural translation helped to naturalise the Bible stories as vernacular tales, in addition to detailing, if not privileging, the domestic landscape. The plays of light on hills, fields, villages and cloud formations were exercises in mood (*stimmung*) as much as topographical realism. Desert stories were re-cast in Northern forest clearings; colours became muted.

Paintings of the Crucifixion achieved their visual tension by uniting the vertical cross, and its human victim, with the horizontality of the landscape, an axial tension which continues to exert a dramatic hold on the Western visual tradition. This is memorably evident in the paintings of Caspar David Friedrich, or in that masterpiece of 20th century landscape architecture, the Stockholm Woodland Cemetery by Gunnar Asplund and Sigurd Lewerentz (with its granite cross locking earth and sky together), as well as in Anthony Gormley's cruciform *Angel of the North*: three very different examples of this enduring morphological trope.

Through repeated use and familiarity, this verticality is now embedded even within secular traditions of visual representation. In photography there are commonly either 'landscape' or 'portrait' formats, neatly exemplifying these two distinct axes. Though Asplund and Lewerentz were both atheists, they nevertheless felt that a large cross was vital to the entry sequence of the now-famous cemetery approach, and Asplund cited the influence of Friedrich's *Cross by the Baltic*, writing that, 'to those who see it as such, a consolation, to those who do not, simply a cross.' Caroline Constant, historian of the Stockholm cemetery, added that 'its stark silhouette could also symbolise the solitude of the 20th-century individual, for whom religion may no longer provide solace.'[9] Gormley's angel, though strongly cruciform, represents a man who has discovered wings, and thus becomes a symbol of hope and freedom.

A phenomenological approach to this issue of the *axis mundi* – the axis by which the human presence establishes itself in the world – is particularly rewarding. The Norwegian architect and historian Christian Norberg-Schulz, a critical interpreter of Heidegger, has written that, 'the *axis mundi* is therefore more than a centre on earth; being a connection between the cosmic realms, it is the place where a breakthrough from one realm to the other can occur.'[10] Thus the vertical is simultaneously the human and the sacred, earth-bound, but reaching up towards the sky. This is what classically the minaret, the tower, the steeple and the cross in the landscape sought to symbolise; today, however, other emblems of human endeavour take their place. As to the horizontal axis, this then is the plane of action, of movement and, over time, the creation of place and dwelling.

This axis remains crucial to the representation of landscape in the modern world. In recent years I have collaborated with two photographers on books about landscape: Larraine Worpole (to whom I'm married) and Jason Orton. Several projects with Orton have evolved from walking expeditions in the erstwhile *terra nullius* of the Thames Estuary and coastal Essex. One of the great challenges for us has been representing these largely deserted places – once the terrain of early settlement, climactic battles, changing agricultural practices, millenarian religious beliefs, large-scale industrial development, housing expansion and economic retreat – as inhabited landscapes, but without necessarily including people in them, believing that the landscape itself should disclose its own history as much as possible. At one point we had to decide whether to include any of the portraits that Jason had taken during these long excursions. Try as we did, we couldn't make these (mostly vertical) portraits fit, for, as we soon came to realise, both Jason's photographic point of view and my essay were based on a sense of distance (though not detachment). Distance of space, distance of time. The portraits brought us too close in, broke the spell, disrupted the topographical reverie we were each trying to create.

This does not mean that the book which resulted from our collaboration, *350 Miles*, was depopulated. The water's edge proved to be for both of us a memory theatre, a place of constant shape-shifting and evocation of past lives. Documenting an absence is, after all, an important obligation for those engaged in forms of artistic representation which seek to honour those famously 'hidden from history'. It is not surprising that such documentation tends towards horizontality, with what is suggested as lying below ground being as important as that remaining above.

The great majority of the people who settled and worked in these marshland and river territories is long dead. Even those who now live in the villages and towns on the coast are rarely found walking the sea walls, traversing the empty yards of former factory complexes, or walking the marshlands in deep winter. The industrialisation of agriculture itself has produced its own eerie depopulation, as landscape historian Nan Fairbrother once observed, noting in a phrase that has haunted me since I first read it, that even 'the animals are coming indoors.'[11]

Yet human traces are everywhere, whether in the exotic ballast flora growing in the vicinity of old ports and harbours, in the derelict jetties, cranes and warehouses of abandoned docks, in industrial ruins, in deserted asylums and hospitals, derelict boats, and a multitude of other *memento mori* of past lives and endeavours. The field systems themselves tell an epic story, with Oliver Rackham reminding us that 'the modern development of South East Essex has all been inserted into a grid laid out nearly 2,000 years ago.'[12] Capturing this palimpsest of past lives and changing landscapes is a key part of a new aesthetic, and represents a formidable challenge to landscape photography, though in the work of photographers such as Jason Orton, Justin Partyka, Simon Read and Jem Southam one can see this challenge being met, all producing as they do images of almost geological intricacy and responsiveness to multiple traces of human dwelling.

There was a time when writers who travelled widely and wrote about the countryside did so by regarding the topography, economy, social and religious life as an integrated whole, even when found archaic or badly wanting. American landscape historian J.B. Jackson has made this point on several occasions, noting that Daniel Defoe, John Evelyn (Jackson's favourite chronicler one suspects), Arthur Young and William Cobbett were all as interested in customs, crafts, agricultural traditions, husbandry and religion as they were in the distinctive flora and fauna of the region, let alone its aesthetic beauty. In Jackson's view this approach was disastrously supplanted by a burgeoning Romantic view of nature which took little or no notice concerning matters of livelihood or human flourishing, concentrating on the effects of landscape on the spectator's sensibility rather than on the felt experience of those who lived and worked in it.

The development of the Picturesque aesthetic in Britain, in conscious rejection of French and Italian formalism, retained some social element in its early formulations, in that it was seen to represent English freedom rather than Continental despotism.[13] Yet even that rationale evaporated as the style became the province of the rich and powerful, happy enough on occasions to clear whole villages and forests in order to achieve a more 'natural' look. Landscape improvement and subsequently aesthetic reception became dominated by painterly and theatrical visual effects, dispensing with notions of utility or economy. Of William Kent, who started out in life as a painter, Walpole wrote that, in his designs, 'he realised the compositions of the greatest masters in painting.' Lancelot 'Capability' Brown said that his ideal was to make the 'English garden exactly fit for the Owner, the Poet and the Painter.'[14] Humphrey Repton was distrusted by many throughout his life as being a showman, a man who used 'before' and 'after' sketches to sell his improvements to wealthy land-owners, with one disillusioned estate steward complaining that Repton's proposals for Longleat amounted to nothing more than 'a Stage trick'.[15]

This may be unfair to a canonical group of landscape designers whose influence continues to this day, and it is certainly true that garden and landscape design is always in its first intimations an exercise in sketching and drawing up plans.[16] Nevertheless, these men were designing what they regarded as private gardens, which such landed estates patently were, and whilst British garden design has continued to exercise a profound influence across the world, with regard to larger public landscapes in the 20th century the influences have mostly been the other way. Today the British look to the Dutch, the Americans and the Scandinavians for imaginative responses to the design of public landscapes, particularly where this involves large-scale land reclamation, or the creation of new ecological parks on the sites of what was once industrial, contaminated land. The gardenesque tradition has had problems in translating itself into a 21st century public works tradition (though Lutyens, Jekyll and the Jellicoes had important successes in this field, particularly in projects involving memorialisation).

Significant elements of the Essex coastal landscape are wholly a product of the modern world, including strategic areas of land reclaimed from the sea, as well as in the fortuitous creation of vast swaths of former industrial and military land now lying unused and neglected. The former was created for agricultural purposes rather than human habitation, since 'draining the swamp' has been fundamental to the construction of modern societies across the world.[17] It was both a product of the Enlightenment and a precursor to many and various imperial colonisation schemes. In the 19th and early 20th centuries Essex provided a home to a variety of metropolitan social reform projects employing the vocabulary of the land colony where, under strict conditions, or in a spirit of political zeal, new lives might be moulded. These included the Hadleigh Farm Colony (founded 1891, Salvation Army), Mayland Colony (1896, Socialist), Purleigh Colony (1896, Tolstoyan Anarchist), Ashingdon Colony (1897, Tolstoyan Anarchist), Wickford Colony (Tolstoyan Socialist) and Laindon Farm Colony (1904, Socialist/Municipal).[18]

Land reclamation schemes commonly symbolised a new world in the making. Such pioneering exercises in hydraulic engineering were followed up with the creation of reservoirs, water towers and pumping stations, electrification schemes requiring power lines and pylons, generating sub-stations, and cola-fired, gas-fired or nuclear power stations. Essex has all of these in abundance, and all brought vast improvements to rural life and amenity. With the exception of a handful of modernist poets in the 1930s who proclaimed the beauty of pylons and the power stations, these new architectural and engineering works have never been formally absorbed into the aesthetic representation of rural life and landscape, and these omissions are still evident.

In a critique of the ruralist magazine *This England*, Tim Edensor takes issue with its editorial policy on photography, noting that 'it is worth speculating about what photographs exclude through the selection of angles and frames, for there are no pylons, mobile phone masts, new buildings or telegraph poles to be seen. These more recent features of the countryside co-exist in the palimpsest of Englishness, but are edited out of the picture.'[19] The deliberate excision or exclusion of the industrial and communications infrastructure which underwrites and sustains rural life today is as politically questionable as the re-writing of history, or the wilful manipulation of photographic images to misrepresent actuality – however much the latter itself is an editorial or compositional construct.

III *All Tomorrow's Landscapes*

British topographical writing in recent years has been dominated by the landscapes of East Anglia, whether in the writings of J.A. Baker, Ronald Blythe, W.G. Sebald, Graham Swift, Andrew Motion, R.F. Langley and Mark Cocker, together with the work of a number of contributors to this book. Earlier writings by Sylvia Townsend Warner, Denise Levertov and Sybil Marshall helped set the scene.[20] If landscape and national identity are uneasy familiars or surrogates of each other, it is worth asking what is Englishness today if its favoured topography is based on the low horizons and cold seas of its eastern approaches? Why does the zeitgeist now favour a lonelier, bleaker, more rebarbative sense of place?

It cannot just be proximity to London. In the late 19th and early 20th centuries a growing number of British artists' colonies preferred to locate themselves as far from industry, commerce and metropolitan life as it was possible to settle.[21] Today the romance of the remote is no longer a part of landscape aesthetic – if anything the opposite is the case. Since the Second World War there has been a growing emphasis on the vernacular and familiar as equally worthy of artistic interest, exemplified in the allotment drawings by John Nash for John Pudney's 1944 collection of seasonal sonnets, *Almanack of Hope* or of Tom Hennell's drawings for C. Henry Warren's *The Land Is Yours*, published in the same year. Like the enormous rise in popularity of birdwatching in this period – another of the arts of peace – these were cultural responses to the post-war democratic settlement. Had Rex Whistler survived the war, his work might have taken the same direction.

Artists such as Eric Ravilious and John Aldridge gravitated towards Edward Bawden in Great Barden, Essex (before and after the war), as well as to Cedric Morris at Benton End in Hadleigh, Suffolk, just over the border, with John Nash living close by. Interestingly, both Bawden and Morris preferred to describe themselves as artist-plantsmen or artist-gardeners. There were also writers' enclaves centred around George Barker and Elizabeth Smart at Tilty Mill, in Essex, or those around Randall Swingler in 'the People's Republic of Pebmarsh', a small Essex village, where artists and intellectuals such as Alan and Isabel Rawsthorne, Humphrey Searle, Paul Hogarth, Edgell Rickword, John Berger and occasionally Hedli and Louis MacNeice collected together at weekends, and where aesthetic principles and concerns were heatedly discussed.[22]

Outsider status still clings to Essex. It is frequently excluded from coffee-table books promoting the picturesque attractions of the other East Anglian counties – Suffolk, Norfolk and Cambridgeshire – whilst never being considered properly one of the 'Home Counties' either. The county is seen to lack respectable heritage and legitimacy, and at least one writer has referred to the redundant industrial sites of the lower Thames, with a degree of admiration and even affection, as 'bastard countryside', borrowing the term from Victor Hugo.[23]

It is the work of the late W.G. Sebald that has been most crucial to the re-imagining of the region. Most importantly Sebald has woven East Anglia back into a European narrative, since his writings are replete with references to the interconnectedness of the eastern shoreline with the dark places of European history. The affinities and correspondences he teases out and interrogates in his travels and memories often begin and end at Liverpool Street station. The gloominess of the old station suffuses several encounters in Sebald's peregrinations, reminding us that Pevsner had, many years before Sebald, attributed the lack of interest in Essex and beyond to the grim disincentive of this then bleakest of London rail terminals.

Because so much of East Anglia is marshland and estuary, sky and water, the chromatic range on the east coast is quite different to that found elsewhere in Britain. Edward Bawden, who, along with Eric Ravilious, adopted Essex and made an art out of its ramshackle farm outhouses, small-holdings and bleak winter fields, said that the approach of spring filled him with horror, knowing that everything would turn green. Both preferred the browns, russets, mauves, greens and muted colours of the furrowed fields, decoy ponds and fens of East Anglia in winter. In doing so they created a sensibility – part aesthetic, part bloody-minded – that contributed an enduring element to the muscular style of 20th century English art.

These unassimilated landscapes need to be recorded and valued if they are not to be wilfully levelled or 'improved' in the name of some larger political programme. What is currently being done in the name of housing development and 'creating new communities' in the 'Thames Gateway' is little short of disastrous. History and meaning are being blown apart, ripped up, flattened and eradicated in a kind of Year Zero approach to development. Little acknowledgement or respect for public memory is evident in these schemes.

One of the most thoughtful critics of the rush to eradicate all memory of the past – in this case in another part of industrial Britain – is the environmentalist and theologian John Rodwell. In his 2006 Reckitt Lecture, *Forgetting the Land*, he spoke of the coalfields of the Dearne Valley, where his grandfather started work in the mines at the age of ten. When Rodwell went to the National Mining Museum seeking archive information about his grandfather's work record, he was told that 'all filing cabinets with all their records, furniture, office buildings and all the other superstructures of a colliery were bulldozed into the shaft.'[24] These shafts were then capped, and in the case of his grandfather's pit, Cortonwood, it 'disappeared as if it had never existed.'

Rodwell recounted the story of Ian Winstanley, a volunteer historian who set up the Coal Mining History Research Centre to 'compile a complete list of the 90,000 or so men, women and children who have lost their lives in mining accidents'. Winstanley is insistent that their names should not be forgotten, and Rodwell describes this as constituting a 'sacramental approach to place', challenging those landscape projects which deny 'former trails of painful happenings, broken promises, unfair demands', and reminding us that 'the ethics of memory are primarily concerned with the relationship between forgetting and forgiving.'

Elsewhere in Europe and North America, progress on re-imagining and bringing back into public esteem such former industrial landscapes is more advanced – as is a respect for the public memory of the sites concerned. Where landscape students used to travel to Stourhead in Wiltshire, Vaux-le-Vicomte in France, or the Boboli Gardens at Bomarzo in Italy to admire the work of the great masters, today's more adventurous trainees visit Gasworks Park on the shore of Lake

Union in Seattle or the Landschaftspark created on the site of the former steelworks in Duisburg-Nord, close to the Ruhr. In Seattle visitors clamber over rusting retorts and towers or join fellow picnickers on the undulating green sward covering industrial spoil, looking out to ageing jetties where cargo-boats once docked. In Duisburg strollers climb the 350 foot high narrow iron-caged ladder to the top of the blast-furnace chimneys or venture along catwalks overlooking the shunting yards. These have been planted as orchards, from where one can watch diving club members descend into the black waters of the former coal bunkers, now flooded. These are the landscapes of the future.

Similar exercises in the sympathetic recuperation and re-enchantment of some of the most blighted parts of post-industrial and de-militarised Essex are now underway. The wildlife reserve at Fingringhoe on the River Colne, created by the Essex Wildlife Trust on the site of former gravel and sand extraction pits, is a personal favourite. There, in high summer, nightingales populate deep avenues of blackthorn and hawthorn and fill the air with constant birdsong; adders can be seen dozing on vacant stretches of sand between large swaths of yellow gorse (with its heady smell of coconut). Fingringhoe is surrounded by army firing ranges, their red warning flags snapping in the estuary breeze; they are for most of the time silent and, collaterally, provide a home to a rich variety of over-wintering ducks, geese and waders, as well as a small colony of seals.

Canvey Wick, on Canvey Island in the Thames Estuary, where my family briefly lived in the 1950s in a plotland bungalow, and often considered one of the ugliest settlements in Britain, is now described as 'England's little brown rainforest', supporting 'more biodiversity per square foot than any other site in the UK.' Another nature reserve has been established on Two Tree Island, close by, a former landfill site where I and other recalcitrant grammar school boys used to meet up at weekends to fire air guns at each other. Today it is richly vegetated and serene. The eastern edge of the island faces on to a series of brackish lagoons that have recently become a principal breeding ground for avocets in Britain. Finally, at Rainham Marshes, another estuarine landscape, lit by a kaleidoscope of cloud, sky and water converging on the Thames as it bends at Erith Rands, yet another wildlife sanctuary has been created. Established on a former collection of military firing ranges and ordnance depots close to Dagenham, the RSPB has brought to fruition a rich marshland environment, where birds arrive from many parts of the world, and the landscape is home to large colonies of marsh frogs, voles and other water creatures, all now breeding successfully.

Despite appearances, the landscape at Rainham has been carefully orchestrated, architecturally and ecologically. Grazing has been restored, saltwater, sweetwater and brackish conditions demarcated and, in many other ways, detailed attention has been paid to recreating historic landscape conditions which originally were responsible for such diverse varieties of flora and fauna. There is an architecturally distinctive visitor centre designed by Van Heyningen and Haward that adds a strong sense of destabilising colour to the river frontage. The complex network of boardwalks, bridges, bird hides and viewing platforms designed by Peter Beard of Landroom has a strong philosophical basis in the art of path-finding and memory of place, weaving in references to pre-historic brushwood riverside tracks (the exquisite carved wooden 'Dagenham Idol' from 2400 BC was found here), the medieval field system and the rusting ruins of military infrastructure – all combined together in a subtle open-air theatre of memory.

Alas nothing like the subtlety and sophistication which modern ecologists and the very best of landscape architects now bring to the laying out and re-planting of wildlife sanctuaries – and the imaginative creation of a new idiom of habitat and flourishing – is given to the crude new housing settlements close by. We are learning to find a home for the birds in these debatable lands, but not ourselves. It doesn't have to be this way.

1. Norman Longmate, *Island Fortress: The Defence of Great Britain 1603–1945* (London: Hutchinson, 1991).
2. Christopher Somerville, *The Other British Islands* (London: Grafton Books, 1990), p.13.
3. David Corke, *The Nature of Essex* (Buckingham: Barracuda Books, 1984), p.35.
4. Cited in Kate Soper, *What Is Nature?* (Oxford: Blackwell, 2001), p. 213.
5. Cited in Kenneth Clarke, *Landscape into Art* (London: John Murray, 1976), p.153.
6. Cited in Julian Barnes, *Nothing to be Frightened of* (London: Cape, 2008), p.48.
7. Kenneth Clarke, *Landscape Into Art*, p.33.
8. All three examples are taken from Kenneth Clark's *Landscape into Art*.
9. Caroline Constant, *The Woodland Cemetery: Toward a Spiritual Landscape* (Stockholm: Byggförlaget, 1994), p.100.
10. Christian Norberg-Schulz, *The Concept of Dwelling* (New York: Electra/Rizzoli, 1985), p.23.
11. Nan Fairbrother, *New Lives, New Landscapes* (Harmondsworth: Penguin Books, 1972), p.73.
12. Oliver Rackham, *The History of the Countryside* (London: Phoenix, 2004), p.161.
13. Horace Walpole, *The History of the Modern Taste in Gardening* (New York: Ursus Press, 1995).
14. These two quotations come from, Fiona Cowell, 'The designed landscape', in L.S. Green (ed.), *The Essex Landscape: In Search of its History* (Essex County Council, 1999).
15. Cited in Stephen Daniels, 'Scenic Transformation and Landscape Improvement: Temporalities in the Garden Design of Humphrey Repton', in Marc Treib (ed.), *Representing Landscape Architecture* (Oxon: Taylor & Francis, 2008), p.47.
16. Marc Treib (ed.), *Representing Landscape Architecture*.
17. David Blackbourne, *The Conquest of Nature: Water, Landscape and the Making of Modern Germany* (London: Cape, 2006).
18. Detailed at www.utopia-britannica.org.uk
19. Tim Edensor, *National Identity, Popular Culture and Everyday Life* (Oxford: Berg, 2002), p.43.
20. For more details on the literary and pictorial recording of the Essex landscape, a good starting point is the 'Memory Maps' website for Essex, a joint initiative by Essex University and the Victoria and Albert Museum, www.vam.ac.uk/activ_events/adult_resources/memory_maps
21. Nina Lübbren, *Rural Artists' Colonies in Europe 1870–1910*.
22. For the Tilty Mill story, see Christopher Barker, 'Life at Tilty Mill', *Granta* 80, 'The Group', Winter 2002. For a very comprehensive account of Pebmarsh, see the chapter, 'The People's Republic of Pebmarsh' in, Andy Croft, *Comrade Heart: A Life of Randall Swingler* (Manchester University Press, 2003).

23. William Mann, '"Bastard Countryside": The Mixed Landscape of London's Lower Lea', Scroope 15, *Cambridge Architecture Journal*, 2003.
24. John Rodwell, 'Forgetting the Land', Reckitt Lecture 2006.

Further Reading

David Blackbourne, *The Conquest of Nature: Water, Landscape and the Making of Modern Germany* (London: Cape, 2006).
Kenneth Clarke, *Landscape Into Art* (London: John Murray, 1976).
Caroline Constant, *The Woodland Cemetery: Toward a Spiritual Landscape* (Stockholm: Byggförlaget, 1994).
David Corke, *The Nature of Essex* (Buckingham: Barracuda Books, 1984).
The Countryside Agency, *Agricultural Landscapes: 33 Years of Change* (Wetherby, 2006).
Andy Croft, *Comrade Heart: A Life of Randall Swingler* (Manchester University Press, 2003).
Gillian Darley, *Villages of Vision: A Study of Strange Utopias* (Nottingham: Five Leaves Publications, 2007).
Tim Edensor, *National Identity, Popular Culture and Everyday Life* (Oxford: Berg, 2002).
Nan Fairbrother, *New Lives, New Landscapes* (Harmondsworth: Penguin Books, 1972).
L.S. Green (ed.), *The Essex Landscape: In Search of its History* (Essex County Council, 1999).
Norman Longmate, *Island Fortress: The Defence of Great Britain 1603–1945* (London: Hutchinson, 1991).
Nina Lübbren, *Rural Artists' Colonies in Europe 1870–1910* (Manchester University Press, 2001).
Robert Macfarlane, *The Wild Places* (London: Granta, 2007).
Christian Norberg-Schulz, *The Concept of Dwelling* (New York: Electra/Rizzoli, 1985).
Jason Orton & Ken Worpole, *350 Miles: An Essex Journey* (Essex County Council, 2005).
Jonathan Raban, *Coasting* (London: Picador, 1987).
Oliver Rackham, *The History of the Countryside* (London: Phoenix, 2004).
John Rodwell, 'Forgetting the Land', Reckitt Lecture 2006.
Donald Scragg, *The Return of the Vikings: The Battle of Maldon 991* (Stroud: Tempus, 2006).
Christopher Somerville, *The Other British Islands* (London: Grafton Books, 1990).
Germander Speedwell, *Soundings from the Estuary* (London Festival of Architecture, 2008).

Marc Treib (ed.), *Representing Landscape Architecture* (Oxon: Taylor & Francis, 2008).

Horace Walpole, *The History of the Modern Taste In Gardening* (New York: Ursus Press, 1995).

Christopher Woodward, *In Ruins* (London: Chatto, 2001).

Ken Worpole, *Last Landscapes: The Architecture of the Cemetery in the West*, with photographs by Larraine Worpole (London: Reaktion Books, 2003).

WHITCHURCH CANONICORUM, DORSET

Votives to St. Wite

by Elisabeth Bletsoe

"true anchoresses are called birds"

        the fluttering heart

titmouse flurry   beats against glass, tinsel
imprisoned under the   claws fretting the leadlight
    upturned boat of the nave

        though the door to the sun/Son
        stands   open

the winged tower
grows budding heads with ex-
ophthalmic eyes   talons & herpetic skin

    vitreous   *where are the angels?*
    shadows

      "sealed in
         yet soaring"

petitions/
        petrous/
                piteous

    heal mi blodi sawle

from me did the all come forth and
unto me did the all extend

       the submerged forest flows
          back to its source, lias

& blue clay fanning out   clay   veins (in the back of my hand)
     bearing twigs, branches, birchbark   & many hazelnuts
           "all laying anyhow"   exhumed by woodmice
      blackened stump
   with adherent leaves/leaf   impressions   washed out

        elephant bones;
          a bowl carved from the alder's
             oracular limb, a wooden bowl &

     antlers in the peat

I am wedded to these woods   this water

      the
   wind's panthalassic echo   surging
   forms the matrix of   & rolling
     my dreams
brands my unforgiving skin   my body
   is becoming this   dirt & fish-scale under my nails
    my assigned place

 billet   socket   groove
   tuck   garth   pen
   fold   close   enclosure
      anchorhold / holdfast
as barley moon   woneth ant waxeth ne
shifts towards blood moon   nis neaver stude-vest

is becoming this   my order of service
    uht-song bi niht i winter
        i sumer the dahunge

translating   observing
  the skywriting of   on a fading epitaph
    fieldfares   thunderflies mating
        impressing
    my palms with yew bark's
      red fracture

split a piece of wood and I am there
lift up the stone and you will find me

    only in silence the word

          this word seggeth

"the structural dome of the Vale strictly
    an elongated oval pericline   (like an upturned boat)"

    & I at the centre of
    a cratch-cradle

of springlines   bridlepaths   & holloways

patterns of drainage
    & incision

    gederith in ower heorte alle seke
      ant sarie
speaking a mass over these worts
    that wa ant poverte tholieth

    for stone & stranguary, for
    soldering the sinew cut   coction/decoction
              in sunder
                  vulnerary   electua
      distilled water drunk   of powdered root a drachm
        with juice & oil of Roses by
          antipathy to Mars
  for scabs and tetters
     foul smelling sores
in a hollow tooth   a wineglass
     with honey to digest the phlegm   removeth
        from the eye the pin & web
for hardness & stoppings   against
          the passions of the heart

      lingua cervina
  moist & uncoiling   in wet meadows
                 hoary with down, the
      salve of hire wunden
                involucre

there is light within a woman of light &
she lights up the whole world; if she
does not shine she is darkness

walking the surf-path in
repeated patternings along the winter beach   storm pilings:
          grating of shingle   the
            upturned hull of a boat
    a rosary of pebbles

receiving under the radar those
ghosted signals from shipping long
confounded   succumbed to
    the hypnotic pull of colder reaches

                        the whale road

continued scourings reveal
        pyritised gleamings   a broken phragmacone
                landslip topography
                        following
                the slumped narrative of the cliffs
                standing
on this the southern coastline's
                        highest point   wind bent
                                        in on itself in the
                                        shape of a thorn
    do you want to hear how it feels?

                the song of the grass   rattle
                        of sea-pinks' dried calices

ther foryeoteth al the world, ther
    beoth al ut of bodi
            ther i sperclinde luve   my thoughts & prayers
                                           up towart heovene
                "cloud-piercing"

                        from knots of conscience
                                smoothing the heart

because thou hast drunk,
thou hast become drunk from the bubbling spring
which I have measured and tended

how close life's surface   imprisoned in my
how tough the membrane that   own time by
traps me beneath   the story of my fate

                the cul of the axe

blinded by vision those
who pilgrimage
are not aware of their journey
    only the passage of time

naket of haliness ant gasteliche wrecche

   their low vehement jarrings
     fanatical griefs, intransigent
          as children   leavings
               of peg-dollies & troll-beads

               forests of wax

       anachorein
       to go   apart

under my tongue the
egg will hatch &
my mouth will give birth   the fluttering heart
   birthing my own soul

   where are the angels?   the timeline
                         becoming a helix

HIC . REQESCT . RELIQUE . SCE. WITE

    the thigh-bones of
     a small woman about
      forty &
    a scattering of teeth

   those are periwinkles that were my eyes

           I am a bird-girl now

YSTRAD FFLUR, CARDIGANSHIRE, WALES

The Grave of Dafydd

by Jay Griffiths

It is Wales and it is raining, raining on the hedgerows, raining on the hills, raining on the rivers, raining on the kingfishers, raining on the grave of that most beloved of the old poets.

Dafydd ap Gwilym is buried at Ystrad Fflur, the flower-strewn vale which shelters the remains of a Cistercian abbey. Just down the road from Ystrad Fflur, or Strata Florida as it is known in Latin, is Pontrhydfendigaid, a village of pebble-dash council estates, parents in too-thin jackets smoking at the school gates, the Spar-boys kicking a can, the nowhere-else-to-go giro days and the chips-with-everything TV nights of rural poverty. There is wealth here, too, in the countryside beyond the towns: the undwellings of second homes. And there are memories of other homes: Dafydd wrote of the 'houses of the glade' where he made love in the surrounding woodlands.

It is an afternoon of late winter, when moss on the abbey's stone walls is damp and bright, and the fiddlehead ferns are tuning up for spring. Dafydd's grave – and, yes, all his readers are on first-name terms with him – is marked by an ancient yew. There are in fact two ancient yews in the churchyard and he may be buried under either, but one in particular is where his memory is now lodged, a focus for his lovers.

Both yews are likely to be some 1,400 years old, predating the abbey itself. Yews can live 3,000 years, and many yew trees in Britain have been here since Roman legionaries used them to shelter from the Welsh rain of 2,000 years ago. Often found in churchyards, yews are, in many traditions, connected with the journey to the underworld, the soul's passage from one life to another; life always, even in death, a generous and regenerative association.

Yews, they say, are 'loners' amongst trees. I prefer to call them soloists, as Dafydd was, a soloist poet and harpist. Dafydd's 14th century contemporary, the poet Gruffydd Gryg, wrote of 'the voice and that great heart' of Dafydd, whose voice still calls, whose heart seems to speak across the years. I am not alone in being a little under his spell; George Borrow, on his walking tour through Wales, knelt and kissed the root of his tree.

Bounded now by a low wall, there are a couple of simple stones to mark his grave, just his name, roughly etched. When I reach his grave, I regret not having brought some gift. Others, heart-enchanted by this poet, have left the odd candle. Lying around on bits of broken concrete, five tipped-over jam jars once held flowers. The flowers are gone and muddy rainwater silts the glass. It is an untidy grave, and therefore full of life. The drains on the chapel-of-rest are more tidily kept than Dafydd's grave and I like that: the church can keep its tidiness.

Fire has burnt out the trunk of the yew – lightning, people say, in a storm in 2002 which struck the tree. Possibly it has also caught fire from a candle left burning in a naughty wind. Please, not deliberate. 'No love shall break you, nor fire consume' writes Gryg speaking to the tree where Dafydd was buried, but it almost has. Almost but not quite, for while flame has hollowed out the yew, yet, living up to all its associations, the yew is still sprouting, greenly alive, rising again, the phoenix from the ashes. Revivification.

> '... And the fire that breaks from thee then, a billion
> Times told lovelier, more dangerous. O my chevalier!
> ... and blue-bleak embers, ah my dear,
> Fall, gall themselves, and gash gold-vermilion.'
> – G.M. Hopkins, from *The Windhover*

After the fire, one arch remains, about the size and shape of a harp. I crawl through it, beneath its twisting striations of yew-wood like the curls of a treble clef, or the waves of smoke in the wind, to sit right inside, leaning back against the heart of the tree, all charcoal now. With that charcoal, I write in a page of my notebook 'Thank you, Dafydd' and tear out the page and bury it. My gift a note. Someone else's gift is a tiny, bleached bone, almost hidden, wedged between two stones in the wall. Fox shit triangulates the grave, a fox-homage which seems entirely apposite for this wild old fox-poet.

Tucked inside the tree's hollow, the wind hardly reaches me and I'm out of the rain. The yew, wrote Gryg, is 'the house where Dafydd is', the tree is 'consecrated for his home'. If it is a home for him, it is an hour-shelter for his visitors, a day-dwelling, a hearth. There is a tradition, around here, of the 'Tŷ unnos', the 'one-night houses' which depended on speed, night and friends. If a person could rig up a house overnight, and have a fire lit with smoke billowing from the chimney by dawn, then they were granted squatters' rights to common land, as far as they could throw an axe to the four directions. Dafydd wrote of the 'house of leaves' he made for his trysts in the woodlands: 'a living-room is better if it grows'.

Like any good hearth, this place seems to offer a long welcome, for it seems to me that Dafydd would have loved people coming to sit by him and have a think. How many come here for a chat with him, I wonder? Or a spliff. Or a kiss. I want to sleep here, my face nudging into his yew-shoulder, as the harp yearns towards Dafydd's chest in the statue of him in Cardiff. (*Play me like your harp, Dafydd*, I can imagine Morfudd chuckling, with Chaucerian sauciness. I would say the same myself, with exactly the same grin.) Dafydd went on a pilgrimage to the Welsh patron saint of lovers, Dwynwen, and asked her to be messenger between himself and Morfudd, a married woman he was deeply in love with, and the subject of so many of his lyric poems. He courted her and made love with her 'under the greenwood tree', according to George Borrow, their handfasting presided over by a bard and friend. It seems fitting for Dafydd who was himself, they say, a lovechild, 'born under a hedge', the wilding son. Morfudd, though, was forced to marry another man, and Dafydd tried to take her back but was imprisoned for his audacity.

Just then, a man opens up a side-gate and comes into the churchyard. For a moment, I'm a little anxious that he has seen me and will tell me to get out of the tree. He walks right up to it, then jumps back startled. He hadn't seen me, and I needn't have worried: it is no concern to him. I apologise, though, for shocking him. 'S'arright, s'arright – I never thought to see anyone sat there, s'all', he says with a wide smile and waves as he leaves.

In the tawny bracken on the hill, light blurs into almost-sun. If I stayed long enough, everything would happen here: an argument, a shag, a snooze, a joke, a day of sunshine. Leaning forward, I realise that the charcoal has traced its black lettering lines over my coat. I've been written on. Ystrad Fflur, or Strata Florida, has a long history of writing. It was a home for manuscripts and hosted resident bards. With the wort-yard herb garden outside, it had a word-yard library inside, and the Abbey brought out an anthology of poetry. Appropriate for Strata Florida, the flowered vale, the word 'anthology' derives from a 'garland of flowers.' The Abbey was noted for its hospitality to poets: dead poets and living poets alike. Dafydd, who is both, is the poet most linked with the abbey, with the surrounding hills and the land beyond.

With five toes and the mysterious heel of a goat, Dafydd leaves his footprints in all the literature and all the woods of Wales. He is thought to have died of the 'Black Death' but he is one of those ancient writers who never died: Montaigne, Omar Khayyam, Ovid, Virgil and Dafydd ap Gwilym. Lascivious, mischievous and hot-blooded, barging his way across more than six centuries, his glad eye catching a girl's glance in a pub, we hear him shout 'fuck' as he bashes his shin in the dark on his way to her room; hitting his head on a table; knocking over a brass bowl; waking the whole innfull of angry men who would suppress his urgings. Irrepressible as the cock of dawn, he writes elsewhere of his fantasy of seducing an abbess, for no other reason than 'because it is May.'

How many men have sung a mock-reproach to their own cock (in English this poem is translated as *The Penis* but surely Dafydd would have talked to it in the vernacular) for the trouble it has caused them? 'You are a trouserful of wantonness... pod of lewdness': lines so vibrant you can still see his rueful smile. 'It is imperative that I become a hermit,' he writes, even as he was rubbing his acorn till it sprouted. When the striking of a wretched clock woke him from an earthy dream, or when a horrible rattlebag of pipes interrupted a shag, we see him bursting with wry frustration all over the page, hundreds of years later. Garrulous, he was, you can tell, as generous in scattering his words as his seeds, invoking the saints to help him in his love affairs, conjuring voices of the greenwood in his love for birds and trees.

He was a troubadour, for sure, and a poet who sung himself into his harp, but something more. He sung himself into the land, asking birds, animals and the wind to carry his messages to all his well-beloveds. More yet: the now-printed words echo the print of his body on the land, as he tells of the way that the places where he made love, the crushed leaves and grass, the bed-shapes under the saplings, will remain imprinted on the landscape forever, and on the landscapes of the heart. He was right, and it is a harpist who confirms it to me. With a copy of Ovid, the great love poet, in his hand, he says, the trace of his lovemaking 'will for evermore be seen', in the 'place of trodden leaves, like Adam's path.'

> 'There is no hillock nor deep hollow
> on either side the valley of Nant-y-Glo
> whose twists and turns my passion does not know'
> – Translated by Rachel Bromwich

❂

By a kind of shamanism of the centuries, he seems to have sung himself into the month of May – his cherished month – with its tumescence of buds and its tumult of green, as if each new-fledged dawn chorus gives him a new-fledged chorus of his own. He was a reveller, rooting for life with all his ruddy geniality, gorging himself on it, eating it and so sharing in its vitality. (And so would I, here at his grave.) He boasts gloriously of his sexuality, and it is easy to imagine he littered the land with offspring, saucy Dafydd a source, a wellspring. The spring was his season, his reason and his emblem, green and cocky as the new leaves of May. He was radiant, too, leaving the land of mid-Wales shining with the light of his love for it, so that even now, here in the lovely, low-down, warm and dirty earth, his words gleam.

In the green valleys, in the high hills, the ages sleep while the old language turns its phrases to describe the land. Penrhyncoch, a 'ruddy promontory', is a fitting place for Dafydd to be born. He wrote in Welsh, Britain's oldest language, one entwined with Latin, and the Abbey's formal inscription to Dafydd is a quote from Virgil, written in Latin and in Welsh.

> 'My heaven-born poet! To me, your song is like sleeping
> On the grass when one is tired, or quenching thirst
> From a gentle brook of sparkling water in the heat.'

❂

This is old land. In geological terms, the oldest stones of Europe are to be found here. The old maps warn you away from Plynlimon, a wild land where even tomorrow is already old, and in its rain shadow, the rain of ages falls, as it always has, ceaseless, changeless, constant, obscuring the velleities of the hills, their slight inclinations, the gentle rise of the will to higher things. It is a land of old animals, too: the last wolves of Britain were thought to have roamed the Powys hills in the 17th century, and badgers, whose very teeth look medieval, are the last of Britain's bears. Last and loathed by many, be it said, and falsely blamed for carrying disease, found mysteriously dead along roads and paths.

Spring, though, is when mid-Wales comes roaring to life. Merry with, drunk with daffodils and their burst of open-hearted sunshine, spring ransacks the land for every bit of glee. In the sky, Dafydd's 'wild untrodden land', skylarks sound the measure of blueness: the bluer the sky, the more they sing. In the woodlands in May, the hedge-music of the finches, sparrows and blackbirds is a realm of its own. It is like listening to Allegri's *Miserere*, before any score of it circulated, when publishing it was banned, when it was only played in spring, in Easter week, in the Sistine Chapel, in the days before fourteen-year-old Mozart's audacious genius wrote out the whole score after just two hearings.

If you sleep out in the woods in spring, the dawn birdsong wakes you, song made sunlight, sunrise made audible. In the dawn chorus, it is hard to know exactly which bird is singing exactly which song: the dawn breeze seems to shake the song from the bird, and the woodland is like an aeolian harp, apparently played by no one except the wind blowing across the strings of the world. 'And what if all of animated nature / Be but organic Harps diversly fram'd' suggested Coleridge, while Shelley, invoking the wind, asked it to 'make me thy lyre, even as the forest is.'

Harp music was the 'craft of the string,' in Dafydd's time, and those strings are unbroken, for the harp has had an uninterrupted history in Wales. Memory, history, the past and the harp seem like ideas strung together in the human mind. Orpheus, the god of music and poetry, played the harp, enchanting humans, animals and gods alike, and with his lyre evoked memory from the underworld past.

When Shakespeare's evil Richard III tells Elizabeth to be silent about his murder of her children, his phrase is 'Harp not on that string, madam, that is past.' She responds: 'Harp on it still shall I till heart-strings break.' For there was, in Shakespeare's time, an idea of the correspondence between the heart's 'strings' of emotion and the actual harp's strings. The strings are metaphoric paths of memory, but harp songs themselves have literally been passed down over the generations, the unbroken strings of time, with harpists memorising music before any notation was used, and it is still a current practice.

Harriet Earis, a British 'harp champion' who lives near Dafydd now, holds history in her hands with the music in her fingers learnt from this oral – and aural – tradition. All the past is not only within the harpist but also the harp, for her harp has a small piece of yew embedded in the frame. It is from that yew tree where Dafydd, the Welsh Orpheus, is buried. Given that molecules of a man will gently snuggle down into the earth, and swim with rainwater when a thirsty tree draws them, then she is, in some infinitesimal but quintessential way, making music which resounds with him: an Orphic resonance, if you'll excuse the pun.

She tells me about going running in the hills of Nant-y-Glo, 'following his call', and I know he has enchanted us both. For myself, why do I love him? In the words of Montaigne: 'Because it was he. Because it was I.' It is my only answer for all my loves.

Dafydd was master of the Welsh poetic form, 'cynghanedd' or 'word-harmony': fluent with its alliteration, assonance and half-rhyme. It is a mesmerising, enchanting and entrancing form, one that Gerard Manley Hopkins was also fluent with, and influenced by. 'As kingfishers catch fire dragonflies draw flame', he wrote in poetry which was partly inspired by Wales: by the Welsh language which he had learned, and by the Welsh landscape where he was dwelling in 1877, his year of miracles, when he wrote most of his best poetry.

The oral transmission of songs, music and poetry is an unbroken path, a kind of songline over time which is known to musicians. The songlines were made famous by Bruce Chatwin, writing of Australian Aboriginal people, but there are aspects of songlines all over the world, a music of the land, passed from singer to singer, held in mind by memory.

I was once told that the Gaelic word *fonn* means 'song' and 'state of mind' and 'land', suggesting the idea of a songline, a song of land, held in mind. Here, the land near Pontrhydfendigaid is criss-crossed with lines and paths and ancient tracks. The three-day pilgrim route, called the Monks' Trod, from Abbey Cwm Hir to Strata Florida, which I walked some years ago, has been sung with feet and with music for hundreds of years. Few people walk these footpaths now, although the aggressive 'Trespassers Will' and 'Private Keep Out' signs, so common just across the border, are not much in evidence here. It is more likely that you'd see a wonky-lettered plea: 'EweS in Lamb Dogs on Lead Please' but the council's rights of way department will tell you that the footpaths which are blocked most vehemently are those which cross the land of second home owners.

If you walk the footpaths of these lands, you'll see kingfishers along the rivers, flashing out 'like shook foil' to borrow Hopkins' term. Farmers are the kingfishers of the land, flashing out along their territory when you walk the footpaths of their lands. A territorial bird, the kingfisher, it may (seen or unseen) accompany you along a stretch of river, stopping at the point which marks a boundary known only to the brilliance of birds. Then the next kingfisher catches the thread of your path. Farmers, consonant with the land, chime with it in its seasons and proclivities: another kind of consonantal chime (as kingfishers catch fire) in the actual world. They have a consonance with the hills and the birds and the language, the choirs for which Wales is famous.

There is an economic consonance, too: fields of thistles speak of a farmer in trouble: the 'tallest thistle competition' at a village fête suggests the sometimes-desperate attempt to snatch the flower of fun from the nettles of despair. The scruffy outbuildings of the smallholdings are ramshackle and untidily alive. Brambles nibble at rusty prams, while a yellow toy tractor is a saucer for rain. Dumpy-bags of cement rubble mooch by mossy feedbags. Cartridge caps punctuate the mud: an old kite is tangled around empty oil drums and blue plastic piping coils around a rusting car door, while a one-legged wheelbarrow whiles away its retirement as a nest for a puppy.

For all their tidiness, the second homes strike a dissonant note in the landscape. But there is really no such thing as a second home. There are homes and there are denyings of homes to others. As one more house is bought as a plaything, one more family is exiled, in these cruel if bloodless clearances: exiled by toys. The only truly hearthless houses are the second homes, for a hearth is not an object but a result: the result of dwelling. Hestia, the Greek goddess of the hearth, will only dwell in one home.

These second homes disenchant the land, blocking the literal footpaths and the metaphoric songlines. Houses and farms, when dwelled in, are small melodies of livelinesses across the hills: the windows are eyes, the doors are mouths. In the second homes, the windows are blinded, the doors are dumb and the chimney pots deaf to the wind. Eyeless. Rigid. A little rigor mortis setting in among the brickwork. The second homes have the tidied perfection of a grave. Tidy as the drains of Strata Florida. The second home owners have bleached the bluebells of their colour, siphoned off the stream and made twilight an investment opportunity as the 'intruder' lights shine like corpse candles into the emptied night. In Welsh, the word *corff* is corpse, and it is the root of the verb *Gorffen*, to finish: what is finished is perfect and dead. These perfect cottage corpses. Dafydd's grave has more life in it, more dwelling.

❂

Dafydd's grave nestles between the Glasffrwd brook and the Teifi river, famous for its salmon. On a windless day, you can hear the Teifi chirruping on the edge of the graveyard. A wellspring, the 'well of the silent grove' (Ffynnon dyffryn tawel) a mile from the Abbey was possibly honoured long before the new religion of Christianity, as many watersources were, suggesting the revivifying waters of life springing from the underground past. The land of mid-Wales has liquid songlines, in its rivers, and my favourite is the little river, the Clywedog, which means 'heard from afar' – sending out into the world its brave signature of significance, though it's little more than a stream. The Clywedog is the underdog of the mid-Wales rivers; it cannot compete with the Severn or Wye, but by god, it will do its best to be heard. I like that in a river: '*Myself* it speaks and spells, Crying *What I do is me: for that I came*' (G.M. Hopkins.)

Alive with sound in spring, a woodpecker knocks a peg into the dawn, hammering 'listen to me', while in the rabbit-rustling and sheep-snufting fields 'no sound is dissonant which tells of Life,' in Coleridge's words, one who had not heard the vile ferocity of the military jets which tear the sky apart with their low-level flight training in these hills. From a fox's point of audience, or an owl's ears, or a deafened robin and silenced wren, this land has more-than-human songlines. In ways beyond our human senses, too, songlines are traceable across these lands. Salmon, quick and other, leap the Teifi and other rivers in their sudden salmon-run days, finding their paths in scent. It is impossible not to respect their mysterious and extraordinary ability to smell in the ocean water the precise trace of water from the exact rivulet of their own home and, following that scent, like a line on a map, doggedly making the journey back home to spawn and die.

The mythic Welsh poet Taliesin was, he wrote, born from a leaping salmon, eaten by his mother, and his poetry is fluent with a riverrun of metamorphosis.

'The second time I was charmed
I was a silver salmon,
I was a hound, I was a stag,
I was a mountain buck.'

This metamorphosis is ancient, Ovidian, full of pre-Christian ideas of rebirth and reincarnation, the spirit re-housed in the dwelling of a cat or a chough or a man, part of the long pagan tradition which softly, stealthily survives. The last time I walked to the source of the Wye, a chaplet of flowers had been tucked by the tiny spring of its source. A local manufacturer of wood stoves gives out a leaflet with hints on wood-burning: don't burn the elder, it says, it is a fairy tree. One local farmer I know adamantly refuses to honour any midwinter festival except the solstice, and this area was full of pagan tales until Methodism tried to hush the story-tellers. The stories live on, if told in quieter voices.

In Dafydd's poetry, the Christian element looks suspiciously well-behaved. Proper. Minding its manners. As if he did it partly to please his parents and partly as a piece of poetic diplomacy: as long as he threw in some churchy numbers, his resplendently pagan poems, where his true poetic – shamanic – heart lies, might be admitted without too much botheration. His tradition is not only that of poet and harpist but also that of the Welsh wise man or woman, the shaman, also known as the 'consuriwr', conjuror, whose work was to con-jure, to bring about, or to constrain by a sacred invocation, to enchant. One who conjures the spirits of the land as Dafydd conjured the mistlethrush, the wind, owl, fox and roebuck. The conjurors were enchanters. Re-enchanters. And were invoked by metaphor and mouth, as the spirit of Dafydd is now.

Snug in his tree, I pull out his poems, to read, to dwell on a while. In the cold, they warm me. 'Poetry first causes dwelling to be dwelling. Poetry is what really lets us dwell', wrote Heidegger. For an exile, a traveller, a soldier, a refugee or the simply unfathomably lost, one book of poetry can be the single most cherished treasure, because it is a pocket hearth.

Poetry is home: a shelter for the soul. Every beloved poem is an hour-shelter or a day-dwelling, a one-night house. Poetry offers a lodging, the smoke from its chimney tells of a hearth indoors and the warmth of habitation. Poetry is snug with welcome, and nested with significance. Poetry is where dwelling wells with meaning; a defence against the arbitrary, where the psyche, seeking a hearth, uncurls and stretches like a kitten. The 18th-century French poet Jean-François Ducis conjured for himself the beloved home in the country that he had always wanted and never had. When he was seventy, he decided to give himself this home, so he wrote little poems to his flower beds, his kitchen-garden, his wood and his wine-cellar. It never existed, except in poetry, and yet, like the best homes, it has provided a warmth and a welcome to those who come upon the image of his inglenook.

The old monks at Ystrad Fflur were kind to poetry, giving it a home – Dafydd more than any, whose grave here is a focus for his memory as a hearth is focus of a room. It is a good word, this 'focus', in its root meaning 'fire', place of fire, the fireful hearth which invites you in. Dafydd's grave is a hearth, a passing-hearth, a way-hearth, with its charred hospitality. His hearth-in-death, his old yew burns like a kingfisher fishing for fire in lively flame, finding the earth, air and fire constituents of the life force, the flame that drives the love of life. Dafydd lives, alive, thriving, green and invoked.

As Omar Khayyam wrote,

'Here with a loaf of bread beneath the bough,
A flask of wine, a book of verse – and thou'.

Sometimes Orpheus is enough. It occurs to me how the yew at Dafydd's grave has been fed, over the years, by his body and here, with the earth partly-peat and root, and partly charcoal from the tree, I take a peck of earth and eat it. Another kind of dispersal, another kind of metamorphosis of earth.

HOLKHAM, NORFOLK

Hevenyssh

by Lavinia Greenlaw

There is no place as airy and dilute
as level or simple.

The earth as once believed
without curve or spin.

So open a view
casts our presence as retraction

no more than salt
a surface concentration

a resting density: marram or pine.
I bring – I do not know – my nature.

A low pull beyond reach.
A slow rush into and into.

How sun is drawn down.
How water solves each length of sand.

And the sky – so vast a gesture
lifts me from my heart

as doth an hevenyssh perfit creature
that down were sent in scornynge of nature.

ISLE OF LEWIS, OUTER HEBRIDES, SCOTLAND

A Counter-Desecration Phrasebook

by Robert Macfarlane

Our task is that of taking up the written word, with all
of its potency, and patiently, carefully, writing language
back into the land.
— David Abram

Epilogue

Five thousand feet below us, The Minch is in an ugly mood. Grey Atlantic water, chevronned with white wave-tops. Our twin-prop plane reaches the east coast of the Isle of Lewis in the Outer Hebrides, and banks north towards Stornoway, bucking as it picks up the cross-buffets of a stiff westerly. The weather is clear, though, and through the port side of the plane I can see the vast tawny expanse of *Mòinteach riabhach*, The Brindled Moor: the several hundred square miles of peat-bog, peat-hag, heather, loch and lochan that Lewis's interior comprises.

Across the aisle from me two women, North American, look out of the window at the moor. One of them laughs. 'We're flying over nothing!', I hear her say.

'Remind me why we've come here?', the other asks.

'We've come to see nothing!'

'Then we have come to the *right* place!'

They press their shoulders together, both laughing now. *Thunk.* The landing gear engages, descends.

'We're about to land on nothing!'

'Hold on tight!'

I *In Which Names Are Spoken*

Seen for the first time, and especially when seen from altitude, the Moor can easily resemble a *terra nullius*, a nowhere-place. It is – as Barry Lopez has observed – 'hard to see deeply into a landscape that, at first glance, appears to be without distinction', and at first glance the Lewis Moor appears distinguished only by its self-similarity.[1] Bog, peat, moor, lochan and more moor. It is mostly flat (though it rises to the low tops of the Barbhas hills), made up mostly of repeating units of terrain, and its colours are motley and subtle. Then there is its size. This is a region whose apparently undifferentiated expanse seems either to return the eye's enquiries unanswered, or to swallow all its attempts at interpretation. Like other extensive lateral landscapes – sand deserts, ice deserts, prairies – it confronts us with difficulties of purchase (how to anchor perception in a context of vastness) and evaluation (how to structure significance in a context of uniformity). Or – to borrow the acronym that Welsh farmers fondly use to describe the hills of the Elan range in mid-Wales – the Moor is MAMBA country: Miles And Miles of Bugger All.

In 2007 a Hebridean friend of mine called Finlay MacLeod, who lives in Shawbost on the north-west coast of Lewis, sent me an extraordinary document. It was entitled *Some Lewis Moorland Terms: A Peat Glossary*. Finlay and three friends had conducted a survey of the language used in three Lewisian townships (Shawbost, Bragar and Shader) to describe and designate the moorland and peat-banks of The Brindled Moor. That the Inuit language allegedly possesses forty words for snow and ice is the most notorious example of fine linguistic discrimination with regard to natural phenomena.[2] But this comes to seem like airy vagueness when compared to the Hebridean Gaelic lexis for peat and peat-moorland. Finlay's *Glossary* ran to four pages and 126 terms. And as that modest 'Some' in its title acknowledged, it was incomplete. 'There's much language to be added to it', one of its co-compilers,

Anne Campbell, told me. 'It represents only three villages' worth of words. I have a friend from South Uist who said that her grandmother would add dozens to it. Every village in the upper islands would have its different phrases to contribute.'

Many of the recorded terms are remarkable for their compressive precision. *Bugha* is 'a green bow-shaped area of moor-grass, formed and contained by the winding of a stream.' *Mòine dhubh* are the 'heavier and darker peats that lie deeper and older into the moor'. *Teine biorach* means 'the flame that runs on top of heather when the moor is burnt during the summer'. *Stèideadh* is 'the act of walling in the sides of loads of peats when they are being transported, such that none will fall off on the way home.' A *rùdhan* is 'a formation of three peat blocks leaned against one another in a pyramidal structure such that wind and sun will hasten the drying of the blocks.' Others are remarkable for their poetry. *Rionnach maoim*, for instance, means 'the shadows cast on the moorland by cumulus clouds moving across the sky on a bright and windy day.' *Èig* refers to 'the quartz crystals on the beds of moorland stream-pools that catch and reflect moonlight, and therefore draw salmon to them in the late summer and autumn'.

That a lexis of such scope and such exactitude has developed is testimony to the intense relationship of labour which has long existed between the inhabitants of the Western Isles and their land: this is, dominantly, a use-language – its development a function of the need to name exactly that which is being done, and done to. That this language should also so readily admit the poetic and the metaphorical to its designations is testimony to the aesthetic relationship that has long existed between the inhabitants of the Western Isles and their land. This is a language of management, but it is also a language of looking, touching and appreciation, and its development is partly a function of the need to love that which is being done, and done to.

I find the *Glossary* to be a deeply moving text – a prose poem, really – and it instantly gives the lie to any perception of the Moor as a *terra nullius*. 'Glossary' – with its hints both of tongue and of gleam – is just the right term for this document's eloquence, and for the substance to which its description is devoted: peat being gleamy as tar when wet, and as dark in its pools as Japanese lacquer. The *Glossary* reveals the Moor to be a terrain so intricate that it has generated a vocabulary devoted to the finessing and division of its perception and practice. A slow capillary creep of knowledge has occurred here, up out of landscape and into language.[3] The result is a lexis so supplely suited to the place being described that it fits it like a skin. Precision and poetry co-exist here: the denotative and the figurative are paired as accomplices rather than as antagonists.

Such fine discrimination operates in Hebridean Gaelic place-names, as well as in descriptive nouns. In the 1990s an English linguist called Richard V. Cox moved to Northern Lewis, taught himself Gaelic, and spent several years retrieving and recording the place-names in a single district on the west coast of Lewis: *Carlabhagh* (Carloway). Carloway contains thirteen townships and around 500 people and is only 58 square miles in area. Cox's awesome resulting work, *The Gaelic Place-Names of Carloway, Isle of Lewis: Their Structure and Significance*, runs to almost 500 pages and details more than 3,000 place-names. Its eleventh section, entitled 'The Onomasticon', lists the hundreds of toponyms that identify 'natural features' of the landscape. Unsurprisingly for such a maritime culture, there is a proliferation of names for coastal features – narrows, currents, indentations, projections, ledges, rock reefs – often of exceptional specificity: *beirgh*, for instance, a loan-word from the Old Norse, refers to 'a promontory or point with a bare, usually vertical rock face and sometimes with a narrow neck to land', while *corran* has the sense of 'rounded point', deriving from its common lexical meaning of 'sickle'.

There are more than twenty different terms for eminences and precipices, depending on the sharpness of the summit and the aspects of the slope. *Sithean*, for instance, deriving from *sith*, 'a faery hill or mound', is a knoll or hillock possessing the qualities which were thought to constitute desirable real estate for the faeries – viz being well-drained, with a distinctive rise, and crowned by green grass. Such qualities also fulfilled the requirements for a good shieling site, and so almost all toponyms including the word *Sithean* indicate shieling locations. Characterful personifications of places also abound: *A' Ghnuig*, for instance, means 'the steep slope of the scowling expression'.[4]

Reading The Onomasticon, you realise that the Gaelic speakers of this landscape inhabit a terrain that is – to borrow a phrase from Proust – 'magnificently surcharged with names'.[5] For centuries, these place-names spilled their poetry into everyday Hebridean life. They anthologised local history, anecdote and myth, binding story to place. They were functional – operating as territory markers and ownership designators. And they also, fascinatingly, worked as navigational aids. Until well into the 1900s, most inhabitants of the Western Isles did not use conventional paper maps, but relied instead on memory maps, learnt on the land and carried in the skull.

These memory maps were facilitated by a wealth of first-hand experience and – in MacLeod's fine phrase – were also 'lit by the mnemonics of words'.[6] For their users, these place-names were part of the internalised landscape necessary for getting from location to location, and for the purpose of guiding others where they needed to go. It is for this reason that so many of the toponyms incorporate what is known in psychology and design as 'affordance' – the quality of an environment or object that allows an individual to perform an action on, to, or with it. So, for instance, a *bealach* is a gap in a ridge or cliff which may be walked through, but the element *bearn* or *beul* in a place-name can suggest an opening that is unlikely to admit human passage, as in *Am Beul Uisg*, 'the gap from which the water gushes'. *Blar a' Chlachain* means 'the plain of the stepping stones'. *Clach an Linc* means 'the rock of the link', indicating a place where boats can safely be tied up, and so on.[7]

These Hebridean toponyms are, then, audaciously accurate but they are also experiential. They arise in part out of the practice of moving through, seeing and using a landscape. To speak out a run of these names is therefore to create a story of travel – an act of sequential naming in which both way-finding and way-faring are implicit. Affinities exist here with the Southern Yukaghir people of Siberia, whereby place-names that index specific landmarks are told in sequence to form stories or 'verbal maps' describing lines of travel for people to follow who have many navigational songs that narrate the unfolding of journeys along rivers (usually the Kolyma). The songs detail currents, rocks, tributaries, and other landmarks associated with stories and myths.[8]

There is also a clear family resemblance with the Aboriginal Australian vision of the 'songlines'. According to this cosmogony, the world was created in an epoch called 'The Dreamtime', when divine beings known as The Ancestors emerged to find the earth a black, flat, featureless place. They began to walk out across this non-place, and as they walked they broke through the crust of the earth and released the sleeping life beneath it, so that the landscape sprang up into being and shape with each pace. As Bruce Chatwin explains it in his flawed but influential account, 'each totemic Aboriginal ancestor, while travelling through the country, was thought to have scattered a trail of words and musical notes along the line of his footprints.'[9] Depending on where they fell, these notes and words became linked with particular landscape features, both large and small. Thus each significant landform was both a tangible object and intangible note or sign – and the Australian desert was, and remains, criss-crossed by dreamtime tracks.

Each of these tracks has a corresponding Song, whose every note in turn corresponds to a significant feature of the track – a rock outcrop or creek junction that it passes, say. The Songs – which were learnt and passed down within the generations of people – were ways of joining up these notes. Some of the songs were short, and contained detailed information about a local area. Others were long songs, and described 'dreamtracks' which extended for hundreds of miles. As Jay Griffiths puts it, each Aboriginal songline exists multiply as 'a map, a mnemonic, a way of thinking and a form of order'.[10]

One of the most influential recent ethnographic works concerning landscape and language is Keith Basso's *Wisdom Sits In Places* (1996), an investigation into the radical situatedness of thought in the Apache people of Western Arizona. Basso spent a decade living and working alongside the Apache inhabitants of a town called Cibecue. He became especially interested in the interconnections of story, place-name, historical sense and the ethical relationships of person to person and person to place. Early in the book, Basso despatches what he calls the 'widely accepted' fallacy in anthropology that place-names operate only as referents. To the Western Apache, place names do refer, indispensably, but they are used and valued for other reasons as well: aesthetically, ethically and musically. The Western Apache understand how powerfully language constructs the human relation to place, and as such they possess, Basso writes, 'a modest capacity for wonder and delight at the large tasks that small words can be made to perform'.[11] In the Apache imagination geography and history are consubstantial. Placeless events are inconceivable, in that everything that happens must happen somewhere, and so history issues from geography in the same way that water issues from a spring: unpredictably but site-specifically.

Basso writes lovingly of the 'handsomely crafted, bold, visual, evocative' imagery of Western Apache place-names, which hold 'ear and eye jointly enthralled':

Tséé Dotł'zh Ténaahijaahá, which translates as Green Rocks Side by Side Jut Down Into Water (designating a group of mossy boulders on the bank of a stream)

Tséé Ditł'ige Naaditiné, which translates as Trail Extends Across Scorched Rocks (designating a crossing at the bottom of a canyon).[12]

Like their Gaelic or Pintubi counterparts, these place-names are distinctive for their descriptive precision. These names are precise in that they implicitly identify a position from which the place is being viewed – an optimal or actual vantage point – such that when the name is spoken, it 'requires that one imagine it as if standing or sitting at a particular spot'.[13] Basso records that this 'precision' is a quality in place-names that is openly appreciated by their Apache users, in that it invites and permits imaginative journeying within a known landscape. At one point, labouring on a fence-building project with two Apache cowboys from Cibecue, Basso listens to one of the men reciting lists of place-names to himself as he strings and then tightens barbed wire between posts. When Basso asks him why he is doing so, the cowboy answers: 'I like to. I ride that way in my mind'.[14]

In all four contexts (Hebridean, Siberian, Australian, South-West American), language is used both to describe and to charm the land. Word as compass and as cantrip. Speech as a way literally to en-chant the land – to sing it back into being, and to sing one's being back into it.

II *In Which Language Is Lost*

The extraordinary place-language of the Outer Hebrides is currently being lost. Gaelic itself is in danger of withering on the tongue: the total number of first-language speakers in the *Gaeltacht* is now just 60,000. Many of those who do still speak Gaelic are increasingly less interested, for obvious reasons, with the intricacies of place-naming or the fine-grained discriminations concerning nature and landscape of which the language is capable. Tim Robinson – writer, mathematician, and deep-mapper of the Gaelic landscapes of the Irish West Coast – has noted how, with each generation in the Irish West, 'some of the place-names are forgotten or become incomprehensible'.[15] Again and again in the Outer Hebrides,

I have been told that younger generations are losing a literacy of the land. Cox remarks that the previously 'important role' of place-names and 'natural' language in the Carloway culture has 'recently' been sharply diminished.[16] MacLeod, writing in 2006, noted that as people's 'working relationship with the moorland [of Lewis] has changed... the keen sense of conservation that went with it has atrophied, as has the language which accompanied that sense.'[17]

What is occurring in Gaelic is occurring in English, too. Increasingly we make do with an impoverished vocabulary for nature and landscape. The nuances that are observed by specialised languages, whether scientific or vernacular, are evaporating from common usage. As more people are brought up in and live in towns and cities, the land beyond the city-fringe has increasingly become understood as consisting of large generic units ('field', 'hill', 'valley', 'wood'). It has become a blandscape. We are increasingly *blasé* about landscape, in the sense that Georg Simmel used that word in his 1903 essay 'The Metropolis and Mental Life', meaning the indifference to the distinction between things.[18] It is not, really, that the natural phenomena and forms themselves are disappearing, only that there are fewer people prepared to or able to name them, and that once they go unnamed they go unseen: language-deficit leads to attention-deficit.

As the vocabulary of nature and landscape falls into desuetude, so too does the knowledge that such vocabulary holds and enables, and so, too, does the ethos that such a vocabulary might embody or encourage. As we further deplete our ability to name, describe and figure particular aspects of our landscapes, our competence for understanding and imagining possible relationships with non-human nature is correspondingly depleted. As the ethno-linguist K. David Harrison puts it, language death means the loss of 'long-cultivated knowledge that has guided human-environment interaction for millennia... accumulated wisdom and observations of generations of people about the natural world, plants, animals, weather, soil. The loss [is] incalculable, the knowledge mostly unrecoverable.'[19]

In late 2008, a new edition of the Oxford Junior Dictionary was published. A sharp-eyed reader noticed – OUP did not advertise its excisions – that there had been a significant culling of words concerning nature. Under pressure, the Press revealed a list of the words it no longer felt to be relevant to a modern-day childhood. The list included *catkin*, *brook*, *minnow*, *acorn*, *buttercup*, *heron*, *almond*, *ash*, *beetroot*, *bray*, *bridle*, *porpoise*, *gooseberry*, *raven*, *blackberry*, *tulip* and *conker*. The words that had shouldered their way into the new edition of the dictionary included *celebrity*, *citizenship*, *bungee-jumping*, *committee*, *compulsory*, *block graph*, *attachment* and *database*. The substitutions – the outdoors and the natural being displaced by the interior and the virtual – were a small but significant symptom of the administered and simulated life that we increasingly live. Children are now adept ecologists of the technoscape, with a dozen words for font-types and emoticons – but with none for the fruit of the chestnut tree or the bramble. A basic language-literacy of nature is falling from us. And what is being lost along with this literacy is something perhaps even more valuable: a kind of language-magic, the power that certain words possess to enchant our imaginative relations with nature and landscape. As the cultural critic Henry Porter observed of the OUP deletions, what had been lost was 'the plain euphonious vocabulary of the natural world – words which do not simply label an object or action but in some mysterious and beautiful way become part of it.'[20]

III *In Which Enchantment Is Practised*

Writing in 1917, Max Weber proposed that disenchantment (*Entzauberung*) was the distinctive injury of modernity (as the death of affect would become the distinctive injury of postmodernity). Weber famously defined disenchantment as 'the knowledge or belief that... there are no mysterious incalculable forces that come into play, but rather that one can, in principle, master all things by calculation'.[21] This disenchantment was a function of the rise of rationalism, which demanded the extirpation of dissenting knowledge-kinds in favour of a single master-principle. It found its expressions not just in behaviour, including the general impulse to the rational and technological control of nature, but also in emotional response. Weber noted the widespread diminishment of what he called 'wonder' – which was for him the hallmark of enchantment, and in which state we are comfortable with not-knowing – and he noted the widespread expansion of 'will', which was for him the hallmark of disenchantment, and in which state we are avid for knowledge and manipulation.[22] In modernity, mastery was usurping mystery.[23]

Certainly, our common language for nature is now such that the things around us do not talk back to us in the ways that they should. As we have enhanced our power to determine nature, so we have rendered it less able to converse with us. We find it hard to imagine nature outside a use-value framework. We have become fluent in analyzing what nature can do *for* us, but lack the language to evoke what it can do *to* us. Martin Heidegger identified this tendency in 1954, observing that the rise of technology and the technological imagination had converted what he called 'the whole universe of beings' into an undifferentiated 'standing reserve' (*Bestand*) of energy, available for any use to which humans choose to put it.[24]

The rise of 'standing reserve' as a concept has bequeathed to us an inadequate and unsatisfying relationship with the natural world, and with ourselves too, because we have to encounter ourselves and our thoughts as mysteries before we encounter them as service-providers. We need things 'to have their own lives if they are to enrich ours.'[25] But allegory as a mode has settled inside us, and thrived. The idea of fungibility has replaced the experience of particularity.

So we need available to us a language or lexis which resists and then reverses that replacement. This is not to suggest that we need adopt either a literal animism or a systematic superstition. Only that by instrumentalizing nature, linguistically and operationally, we have stunned the earth out of enchantment.[26] And language is vital to the possibility of re-enchantment. For language does not just record experience stenographically, it produces it. Language's structures and colours are inseparable from the feelings we create in relation to situations, to others and to places.[27] Language carries a formative as well as an informative impulse – the power known to literary criticism and linguistic theory as 'illocutionary'.

Certain kinds of language can restore a measure of wonder to our relations with nature. Others can offer small tools for small place-making. Others can allow the things around us to talk to or look back at us, freed from their role as standing reserve, and instead possessing what the early anthropologist Lucien Lévy-Bruhl called 'participation', by which term he designated the animistic logic of people for whom inert objects like stones or mountains are thought to be alive, and for whom certain names or words, spoken aloud, 'may be felt to influence at a distance the things or beings that they name, such that people, places and creatures may all be felt to *participate* in one another's existence, influencing each other and being influenced in turn.'[28] Lopez again: 'One must wait for the moment when the thing – the hill, the tarn, the lunette, the kiss tank, the caliche flat, the bajada – ceases to be a thing and becomes something that knows we are there.'[29]

Between 2002 and 2006, a group of American writers and researchers compiled and published a massive work of place-language, entitled *Home Ground: Language for an American Landscape*. Its ambition was to retrieve, define and organise nearly 1,000 terms and words for specific aspects of landscape. Its ethical presumption was that having a language for natural places is vital for two reasons: because it allows us to speak clearly about such places, and because it allows us to fall into the kind of intimacy with such places which might also go by the name of love or enchantment, and out of which might arise care and good sense. They defined and located their terms, and illustrated them with usages from American literature, science and art. The result, as with MacLeod's glossary, is a kind of sustained prose-poem, exquisite in its precision and its metaphors. It does not so much define as evoke, or it defines through evocation. 'That rivers and streams seldom flow naturally in straight lines is a gift of beauty. Otherwise we would not have canyons that bear the shape of moving water', begins the entry for 'gooseneck', meaning those 'deeply entrenched river meanders... so tight in succession that their bows nearly meet one another'.[30] 'Cowbelly' describes super-soft, finely particular river mud: 'it is along the banks of slow-moving creeks, where the current slackens completely, that the very finest particles of sediment settle out of the water... at the boundary where water becomes silt, the bottom is so plush that the sinking foot of the barefoot wader barely registers the new medium, only a second change of temperature' (a finely particular definition for a finely particulate phenomenon).[31] 'Shinnery' is 'a type of low brush thicket... difficult or impossible to cross on foot or horseback... taking its name from the shin oak (*Quercus havardii*).'[32]

So this dictionary proceeds – lyrically, exactly, enchantingly – supplying and renewing a language of place. The aim of *Home Ground*, wrote Lopez in the introductory essay to the volume, was 'to recall and to explore (such) language... because we believed in an acquaintance with it, that using it, to say more clearly and precisely what we mean, would bring us a certain kind of relief... would draw us closer to... landscapes'. The book sought to make available a vocabulary for 'expressing allegiance and intimacy with (one's) chosen places.'[33] This is the language, Lopez concluded, that 'keeps us from slipping off into abstract space'.[34]

Certainly, the separation of knowledge and nature moves us slowly towards a society in which it is increasingly unnecessary for us to be aware of where we live, beyond the housekeeping of our own private zones. Once this awareness has lapsed, then landscapes beyond those precincts become much easier to manipulate for ill. Good language, used well, can provide a stay against homogenization and against a failure of discrimination, and re-learning a language that holds life in place is now an urgent task. For, once a landscape goes undescribed and therefore unregarded, it becomes more vulnerable to unwise use or improper action.

This is what happened to the Moor of Lewis six years ago.

IV *In Which Songlines Are Sung*

In November 2004, the engineering company AMEC, in conjunction with British Energy, filed an application to build Europe's largest on-shore wind-farm on Lewis. The proposed farm consisted of 234 wind turbines, each of them 140 metres high (more than twice the height of Nelson's Column) and with a blade-span of more than 80 metres (longer than a Boeing 747 measured nose-to-tail). Each turbine would be sunk into a foundation of 700 cubic metres of concrete. The generated energy was to be ducted off the island and down to the 'centres of need' by 210 pylons, each 26 metres high, joined by overhead lines. To service the turbines and pylons, 104 miles of roads would be built, as well as nine electrical substations. Five new rock quarries would be opened, and four concrete batching plants established.

In total, around 5 million cubic metres of rock and 2.5 million cubic metres of peat would be excavated and displaced. All of this was to occur on The Brindled Moor. By AMEC's own admission in their initial application, 'the effect on the landscape resource, character and perception (of Lewis would be) major and long-term'. AMEC's application began a three-and-a-half year battle over the nature and the future of the Moor, primarily between the Outer Hebrideans themselves – around 80% of the inhabitants of Lewis expressed opposition to the plans – and AMEC together with its political supporters.

The crux of the debate concerned the perceived nature and worth of the Moor itself, and the language that was used – and available – to describe it. It was, understandably, in the interests of AMEC and its supporters to characterize the Moor as a wasteland. The metaphors used by the pro-farm lobby to describe the Moor repeatedly implied barrenness. One pro-farm local counsellor dismissed the island's interior as 'a wilderness', suggesting a space both empty of life and hostile in its asperities (wilderness in the old American-Puritan sense of the word, then, or that implied by the desert 'wilderness of Zin' through which the Israelites wander in *Exodus*).

If the pro-Farm lobby charged the Moor with an affective power, it was with the capacity to depress and oppress the human mind. The writer Ian Jack, arguing in support of AMEC's application, described 'Lewis's interior' as 'a vast, dead place: dark brown moors and black lochs under a grey sky, all swept by a chill wet wind'.[35] Jack's comment, like those of the two Americans I overheard on the plane, has precedents in earlier modern encounters with moors: Daniel Defoe, for instance, who in 1725 rode over the ling moors above Chatsworth in Derbyshire, and found them 'abominable', 'a waste and a howling wilderness'.[36] It also recalls the many 19th-century white settler accounts of the Australian desert interior as a 'hideous blank'. 'Everywhere the same dreadful, dreary, dismal desert', lamented the *Argus* newspaper of Melbourne in an 1867 editorial against the 'interior'.

The American geographer Yi Fu Tuan has noted that 'it is precisely what is invisible in the land that makes what is merely empty space to one person, a place to another'.[37] The task that faced the Lewisians, when the conflict with AMEC began, was to find ways of expressing the Moor's 'invisible' content: the use-histories, imaginative shapes, natural forms and cultural visions it had inspired; the ways it had been written into language and memory. They needed to create an account of the Moor as 'home ground', and for that they needed to renew its place-language. 'Those who wish to explain to politicians and others why landscape should be nurtured and made safe for all living things face a daunting task where the necessary concepts and vocabulary are not to hand', wrote Finlay MacLeod in a public essay in 2005. 'It is therefore difficult to make a case for conservation without sounding either wet or extreme.'[38]

So it was that, beginning in early 2005, the islanders began to devise ways of re-enchanting the Moor. They started both to salvage and to make accounts – narrative, poetic, lyric, painterly, photographic, historical, cartographical – which taken in sum or interleaved might restore both particularity and mystery to the Moor, and thus counter Jack's vision of it as a 'vast, dead place'. One of the most memorable moor-works to emerge out of this period of resistance by the islanders was made by two Lewisian artists, Anne Campbell and Jon MacLeod, and entitled *A-mach an Gleann*, or 'A Known Wilderness'. Campbell's family had lived in the township of Bragar for generations, and she and MacLeod wanted to evoke a sense of the Moor as a wild place, home to wildlings, but also to demonstrate how enmeshed it was with human culture. They became interested in the crisscrossing paths and tracks that exist on the Moor (both human and animal in genesis) each of which they saw as a storyline of a kind.

So they began to map their own moor-walks, recording paths taken and events that occurred or were observed along the way. On 27th June 2005, for instance, they walked between '*An Talamh Briste, Na Feadanan Gorma, Gleann Shuainagadail*, and *Loch an Ois*', and saw in these places 'drifts of sparkling bog-cotton', 'scarlet damselflies', 'a long wind, carrying bird-calls'. They 'crossed a greenshank territory' and 'disturbed a hind in long grass', before 'stopping at a shieling where an eagle had preened'. Campbell also documented how, when walking as a child to look for the sheep with her father, he would point out names and features along the way: offering stories of each shieling, stock wall, cairn, stepping-stones, fish-trap and salmon pool. MacLeod delved further back, making speculative reconstructions of atavistic memory maps: 'of the people who traversed this landscape before and after the peat grew, naming features to navigate their way around, or to commemorate stories and people'. In these ways, Campbell and MacLeod began to create their own repertoire of songlines – ancient, modern and new – for the Moor.[39]

Another group of islanders collected and archived poems, ballads, folksongs and testimonies concerning the Moor, mostly from the nineteenth and earlier 20th centuries, including Padraig Campbell's *The Skylark* and Derek Thompson's *The Side of the Hill* and *The Moor*. These were texts written on the Moor in both senses, offering accesses to and of its subtlety. It was in this context that Finlay and his collaborators created the *Peat Glossary*. In spirit if not in form, the *Glossary* is kindred with Hugh MacDiarmid's angry poetic rebuke to an unnamed 'fool' who has dismissed Scotland as 'small'.

'Scotland small? Our multiform, our infinite Scotland *small*?', begins his poem, indignantly. 'Only as a patch of hillside may be a cliché corner / To a fool who cries "Nothing but heather!"'

Taking that patch of hillside as his synecdoche for Scotland, MacDiarmid's poem 'gazes' hard at it, through a poetic loupe, tweezering out this and that for our attention. He finds in the moor 'not only heather' but also blueberries (green, scarlet, blue), bog-myrtle (sage-green), tormentil (golden), milkworts ('blue as summer skies') flourishing on the patches that sheep have grazed bare, down in the unworked peat-hags, sphagnum mosses (yellow, green and pink), sundew and butterwort, nodding harebells that 'vie in their colour' with the butterflies that alight on them, and stunted rowan saplings with their 'harsh dry leaves'. "Nothing but heather!', the poem mocks sharply at its close, 'How marvellously descriptive! And incomplete'.[40]

Finally, the Lewisians also produced a series of what are known in the curious language of planning as 'precognitions' (a 'precognition' is a written statement of the evidence that a witness will give at an enquiry). Scores of precognitions were submitted by the islanders, many of them evocative and dignified in their tones. One such, for instance, was written by Alice Starmore, concerning her long-standing relationship with the Barvas hills of the Brindled Moor. Her testimony included photographs, love songs, and personal stories of her family's exile from and return to the Moor during the 19th century. Starmore wrote that she wanted to convey 'the sense of intimacy about the moor that comes from walking it and working it.'

Her precognition, like so many of those submitted, found the lexis and thought-structures of cost-benefit analysis insufficient to the task of evaluating the Moor – and so took up other registers.[41] 'What is required', Finlay wrote in an appeal to save the Moor, 'is a new nomenclature of landscape and how we relate to it, so that conservation becomes a natural form of human awareness, and so that it ceases to be under-written and under-appreciated and thus readily vulnerable to desecration. What is needed,' he concluded magnificently, 'is a Counter-Desecration Phrasebook'.[42]

He and his fellow islanders worked to produce that Phrasebook, or at least to restore the possibility of its existence. After three and a half years the Scottish Executive ruled on AMEC's proposal. Taking into consideration the protective designations that the Moor possessed (including a UN RAMSAR designation), and the protests against the development (which included 10,924 letters of objection), it decided to reject AMEC's application. The Moor was, at least temporarily, saved.

V   *In Which a Baroque Fantasia Is Imagined*

We need now, urgently, a Counter-Desecration Phrasebook that would comprehend the world. A vast Glossary of Enchantment for the whole earth, that would allow nature to talk back to us and would help us to listen. That would provide us with the necessary tools for responsible place-making. That would keep us from slipping off into abstract space – and keep us from all that would follow from such a slip.

Such a Phrasebook, as I imagine it – and it can exist only as thought-experiment, as baroque fantasia – would stand not as a competitor to scientific knowledge and ecological analysis, but as their supplement and ally. We need to know how nature proceeds, of course, but we need also to keep enchantment alive in our descriptions of nature: to provide celebrations of not-quite-knowing, of wonder, of mystification. Lopez once more: 'something emotive abides in the land, and... it can be recognized and evoked even if it cannot be thoroughly plumbed... [something that is] inaccessible to the analytic researcher, and invisible to the ironist'.[43]

Like Lopez, I am drawn to this idea of a valuable superfluity in nature: a content to landscape that exceeds the propositional and that fails to show up on the usual radar sweeps (but which may be expressible, or at least gesturable-towards, in certain kinds of language). I relish the etymology of our word 'thing' – that sturdy term of designation, that robust everyday indicator of the empirical – whereby in Old English 'thing' does not only designate a material object, but can also denote 'a narrative not fully known', or indicate 'the unknowability of larger chains of events'.[44]

As I imagine it, futilely, this Phrasebook would be filled with language that is – as the American poet Marianne Moore put it in a remarkable essay of 1944 entitled 'Feeling and Precision' – 'galvanized against inertia', where that 'galvanized' carries its sense of flowing current, of jolt and energy received by contact, of circuitry completed.[45] For Moore, precision of language was crucial to this galvanism. 'Precision', she wrote (in a phrase with which I could not be more in agreement), 'is a thing of the imagination' and produces 'writing of maximum force'.[46] Precision here should not be taken as cognate with scientific language, nor as a synonym for pure denotation.

Precision, in Moore's account, is a kind of testimony or bearing witness, which is quite different to rational understanding. It involves not probing for answers, but watching and waiting. And precision, for Moore, is best enabled by metaphor: another reminder that metaphor is not just something that adorns thought, but that it is, substantively, thought itself. Writers must be, she concludes superbly, 'as clear as our natural reticence allows us to be', where 'reticence' mutely reminds us of its etymology from the Latin *tacere*, 'to be silent, to keep silent'.[47] I recall Charles Simic: 'For knowledge, add; for wisdom, take away'.[48]

This unfeasible Phrasebook would help us to understand that as well as thinking *about* landscape and nature, we think *with* it, and, more radically still, that we are thought *by* it. It would be alert to the ways in which cognition is site-specific, in which certain landscapes can hold certain thoughts as they hold certain species or minerals. It would celebrate the fact that there are natural places that present possibilities of thinking and feeling that are otherwise unavailable or elsewhere absent. Such places make our thinking possible, and leave our thinking changed. One recalls here Edward Thomas's description of the thrushes in his late poem *March*: 'Something they knew—I also, while they sang / And after'.[49]

In this respect the Phrasebook would speak with what linguistics calls the 'middle voice': that grammatical diathesis which – by hovering between the active and the passive – can infuse inanimate objects with sentience and so evoke a sense of reciprocal perception between human and non-human.[50] It would possess, too, the memorious alertness of Jorge Luis Borges's character Ireneo Funes, who develops perfect recall after a riding accident. 'John Locke, in the 17th century, postulated (and rejected) an impossible language in which each individual thing, each stone, each bird and each branch, would have its own name', wrote Borges there. 'Funes once projected an analogous language, but discarded it because it seemed too general to him, too ambiguous. In fact, Funes remembered not only every leaf of every tree of every wood, but also every one of the times he had perceived or imagined it ...'.[51]

This hopelessly unwritable Phrasebook would find ways of outflanking the cost-benefit framework within which, unwittingly, we do so much of our thinking about nature. Again and again when we are brought short by natural beauty – the helix of a raptor's ascent on a thermal; a flock of knots shoaling over an estuary; a mountain white-out so pure and even that it abolishes all directions except those indicated by gravity; the shadows of cumulus clouds moving across Lewisian moorland on a sunny day – the astonishment we feel concerns a gift freely given; natural potlatch. During such encounters, we briefly return to a pre-economical state in which things can be encountered 'in their facialities and tendered – that is treated with tenderness – because of the generosity of their self-giving, as if alterity were itself pure gift.'[52]

Indeed above all, perhaps, this impossible Phrasebook would speak the language of tact and of tenderness. The Canadian poet and philosopher Jan Zwicky has written of the importance of 'having language to hand' in our dealings with the natural world, and there is a reminder in her phrase of the relationship between tactfulness and tactility, between touch and ethics.[53] Etymology, as always, illuminates. *Tact: 1(a).* 'The sense of touch, the act of touching or handling.' *1(b)* 'A keen faculty of perception or discrimination likened to the sense of touch'. *2(b)* 'Musicologically, a stroke in beating time which "directs the equalitie of the measure" (John Downland, writing in 1609, translating Andreas Ornithoparcus)'.[54] Tact as due attention, as a tenderness of encounter, as rightful tactility.[55] Tactful language, then, would be language which sings (is lyric), which touches (is born of contact with the lived and felt world) and which touches (affects), and which keeps time, recommending an equality of measure.

1. Barry Lopez (ed.), *Home Ground: Language for an American Landscape* (San Antonio: Trinity University Press, 2006), p. xxi.
2. Notorious in so far as it is untrue. While Inuit does not have forty words for snow (or four hundred, as has also been claimed), it does possess an evocative and discriminatory snow-vocabulary: *pukak* means 'snow like salt', for instance, *massalerauvok* means 'snow filled with water', which is not the same as *mangokpok* ('watery snow'), and so forth. The forty-words-for-snow factoid is so viral within discussions of language-reality and the Sapir-Whorf hypothesis that fatigued linguists have coined the term 'snowclone' to designate its spurious use.
3. As has occurred in many other languages where people have spent generations inhabiting a particular ecological niche and practicing a particular lifeway. The Marovo people of the Philippines, for instance, have a rich language for classifying the schooling manners of fish; the lexis includes *ukuka*, which designates 'the behaviour of groups of fish when individuals drift, circle and float as if drunk' and *sakoto*, meaning 'quiet, almost motionless resting schools of certain fish looking like a gathering of mourners'. The Tuvan language spoken by Siberian nomads is peculiarly attentive to the aural properties of the boreal landscape: *chyzr-chyzr* means 'the sound of tree-tops moving, swaying, cracking or snapping as a result of bears marking trees by clawing at them and by scratching their backs up against them', *koyurt* is the sound of 'human feet treading deep snow', and *hir-hir* is 'both the crackling of a campfire or the sudden rustling of a grouse's wings in the grass.' See K. David Harrison, *When Languages Die: The Extinction of the World's Languages and the Erosion of Human Knowledge* (Oxford: OUP, 2007), p. 50, p. 125.
4. Richard V. Cox, *The Gaelic Place-Names of Carloway, Isle of Lewis: Their Structure and Significance* (Dublin: Dublin Institute For Advanced Studies, 2002), pp. 69–85.
5. Marcel Proust, *Swann's Way* (New York: Henry Holt, 1922), p. 437.
6. Finlay MacLeod (ed.), *Togail Tir/Marking Time: The Map of the Western Isles* (Stornoway: Acair and An Lanntair, 1989), 'Preface', p. ii.
7. Cox, *Gaelic Place-Names*, pp. 69–85, passim.
8. Harrison, *When Languages Die*, pp. 109–11.
9. Bruce Chatwin, *The Songlines* (London: Cape, 1987), p. 13.
10. Jay Griffiths, *Wild* (London: Penguin, 2007), p. 251.
11. Keith H. Basso, *Wisdom Sits in Places: Landscape and Language among the Western Apache* (Albuquerque: University of New Mexico, 1996), p. 44.
12. Basso, *Wisdom*, p. 23.
13. Basso, *Wisdom*, p. 89.
14. Basso, *Wisdom*, pp. 45–46.
15. See Tim Robinson, *Setting Foot on the Shores of Connemara* (Dublin: Lilliput Press, 1996), p. 3; also Tim Robinson, *Stones of Aran: Pilgrimage* (New York: NYRB, 2008), pp. 13–14.
16. Finlay MacLeod, 'Counter-Desecration Phrasebook Needed', *Stornoway Gazette*, 14 February 2008.

17. Cox, *Gaelic Place-Names*, 'Preface', p. i.
18. Georg Simmel, 'The Metropolis and Mental Life', in *On Individuality and Social Forms* (Chicago: University of Chicago Press, 1971), p. 329. For Simmel, *blasé*-ness was a function in part of the numbing effect on perception that the 'shocks' of modernity had administered to the subject, and partly a function of the rise of the capitalist use-value model, which leads to what Theodor Adorno called 'a generalised equivalence of all things'.
19. Harrison, *When Languages Die*, p. 17.
20. Henry Porter, 'The Pity of A Child's Dictionary', *Observer*, 14 December 2008.
21. Max Weber, *From Max Weber: Essays in Sociology*, trans. and ed. by H.H. Gerth and C. Wright Mills (Oxford: Oxford University Press, 1946), p. 139.
22. I draw here on Patrick Curry's illuminating discussion of enchantment and its 'immiscible' relation to modernity, in Patrick Curry, 'On Not Saving Enchantment For Modernity (Even As Religion)', forthcoming in Tom Crook and Mathew Feldman (eds.), *Sacred Modernities: Rethinking Modernity in a Post-Secular Age* (London: Continuum, 2011).
23. Writing four years before Weber, in a chapter of *Swann's Way* (1913) on place-names and place-relations, Proust made a similar distinction between the rise of the scientific and wilful, and the retreat of the unintended and enchanting: '[There are] those natural phenomena from which our comfort or our health can derive... an accidental... benefit', until 'the day when science takes control of them, and, producing them at will, places in our hands the power to order their appearance, withdrawn from the tutelage and independent of the consent of chance.' Proust, *Swann's Way*, p. 438.
24. Martin Heidegger, 'The Question Concerning Technology,' in *Basic Writings*, ed. David Krell (New York: HarperCollins, 1993), p. 325.
25. Tom Gilliver, personal communication. I am indebted throughout this paragraph to Gilliver for ongoing conversations concerning these ideas.
26. See Peter Larkin, 'Scarcely On The Way: The Starkness Of Things In Sacral Space', at http://intercapillaryspace.blogspot.com/2010/03/scarcely-on-way-starkness-of-things-in.html (accessed 08/06/2010).
27. This is not an uncritical restatement of the Sapir-Whorf hypothesis. The Sapir-Whorf hypothesis holds true only in a moderate form: i.e. that vocabulary and grammar affects the ways we perceive things and the ways we recall them (but not that their alteration can perform a radical restructuring of our cognitive equipment).
28. David Abram, *The Spell of the Sensuous: Perception and Language in a More than Human World* (New York: Pantheon, 1996), p. 57.
29. Lopez, *Home Ground*, p. xviii.
30. *Home Ground*, p. 159.
31. *Home Ground*, pp. 89–90.
32. *Home Ground*, p. 325.
33. Lopez, *Home Ground*, p. xvi

34. Lopez, *Home Ground*, p. xxiii
35. Ian Jack, 'Breathing Space', *Guardian*, 26 July 2006.
36. Daniel Defoe, *A Tour Thro' the Whole Island of Great Britain, Divided into Circuits or Journies* (3 vols, 1724–26), III, p. 74.
37. Yi Fu Tuan, *Tòpophilia* (New Jersey: Prentice Hall, 1974), p. 122.
38. MacLeod, 'Counter-Desecration Phrasebook'.
39. Anne Campbell and Jon MacLeod, *A-mach an Gleann*, privately published (Stornoway, 2007).
40. Hugh MacDiarmid, 'Scotland Small?', in *Selected Poetry*, ed. Alan Riach and Michael Grieve (New York: New Directions, 1992), p. 198.
41. See Alice Starmore, *Mamba*, exhibition catalogue (Stornoway: An Lanntair, 2008), passim.
42. MacLeod, 'Counter-Desecration Phrasebook'.
43. Lopez, *Home Ground*, p. xviii.
44. See Adam Potkay, 'Wordsworth and the Ethics of Things', *PMLA* 123.2 (2008): 390–404, 394. This deep-buried meaning of the word 'thing' is likely to be a residue of the Old Danish 'Thing' as designating a community meeting where legal issues were disputed and settled; a parliament or a court. In such a context, the idea of a 'Thing' bears within it a judicial space of uncertainty, the connotation of a matter whose resolution has yet to be determined, is still to be settled.
45. Marianne Moore, 'Feeling and Precision', *The Sewanee Review*, vol. 52, no. 4 (Oct–Dec 1944), 499–507, 500.
46. Moore, 'Precision', 500.
47. Moore, 'Precision', 499. I am compelled, too, by Moore's fanaticism for rhythm as a kind of cognition, a kind of precision: 'it [the effect] begins far back of the beat, so that you don't see when the down beat comes. It was started such a long distance ahead, it makes it possible to be exact'. Moore, 'Precision', 499–500. Here, again, exactitude and knowledge are left, if not quite antonymic, certainly not synonymous.
48. Charles Simic, quoted by Jan Zwicky in *Wisdom and Metaphor* (Kentville: Gaspereau Press, 2005), p. 74. I am grateful to Patrick Curry for introducing me to Zwicky's work.
49. Edward Thomas, *The Annotated Collected Poems*, ed. Edna Longley (Newcastle: Bloodaxe, 2008), p. 35.
50. See John Llewellyn, *The Middle Voice of Ecological Conscience* (New York: St. Martin's Press, 1991).
51. Jorge Luis Borges, 'Funes The Memorious', in *Labyrinths: Selected Stories and Other Writings* (New York: New Directions, 1964), p. 65.
52. Potkay, 'Ethics of Things', 401. Potkay is drawing on the work of Sylvia Benso. See also Larkin, 'Scarcely On The Way'.
53. Zwicky, *Wisdom and Metaphor*, p. 32.
54. *OED* online, 2nd edn (Oxford: 1989).
55. See Valentine Cunningham, *Reading After Theory* (Oxford: Wiley-Blackwell, 2001).

ASHPRINGTON, DEVON

Crow Meadow

by Alice Oswald

I said the buttercups burn in Crow Meadow
Brighter than an arc lamp
I said those buttercups those shining pleading faces
Are also their genitals
I said God how they've grown in one week
Too tall for their clothes

I said look look
Have you seen the bulls in Crow Meadow
Up to their balls in buttercups
I said help have you seen them
Wading in slow surrender like musclemen in drag
Those exhausted bulls eating their weight in gold

She said that's nothing my darling
You should hear them bellowing at night
She said you should hear that huge falsetto grief
It breaks my heart into leaf

On Rona

by Kathleen Jamie

Far over the horizon, out in the north Atlantic, where one might expect a clear run to Iceland or even Labrador, or, if anything, just a guano-streaked gull-slum, the island of Rona is one last green hill rising from the waves.

Or so they tell me. It's forty miles out, several hours sailing, but pretty soon I was prostrate on the aft deck, shivering under the wind- and engine-noise. From deep in my sick cocoon I heard the others calling they could see Rona on the horizon, then more salt, cold, immobilised ages passed until the boat slowed, the wind-rush dropped. When they cut the engines and sent down the anchor, I felt gratitude, but then the boat began wallowing. Worse than the leaping waves was that awful wallowing. There were guillemots though, their cries echoing as though they were stuck down a well, because we were in the shelter of a geo – a steep-sided inlet. Dark cliffs on either side, a rattling as the dinghy was lowered, and voices, one, a man's saying, 'let's get her ashore'.

I must have jumped and scrambled up the slabby rocks as per instructions, and when I met grass, collapsed on it. A green unheaving bosom. Blessed deep core of steady rock, reaching down, down.

Lay there till the nausea passed, and the shivering. Coming back to myself, I heard land-birds, starlings, rolled over, looked up at the sky, smelled a sweet smell, some kind of wildflower, thrift maybe. How lush the grass I lay on; that surprised me. Lush-long and harsh at once. The sky was high and bright with fleet clouds. Lay there, as slowly the sun and breeze dried my waterproofs. Bob the skipper blew the boat's horn as he left, then Stuart and Jill appeared up from the shore, grinning, laden with gear, and we were on our own.

So, for a short while last summer we had Rona to ourselves. Alone in the encircling ocean, me and my companions Stuart Murray and Jill Harden. Stuart's of that sterling tradition of self-taught naturalists; a bird-man who says, 'believe what you see', but a prerequisite of that believing is a great accuracy of seeing, and a rough idea of what you're looking at. For him Rona was an old and beloved haunt, he had brought notes in his own hand from thirty years before; lists and columns of figures pertaining to puffin colonies, to black back gulls and storm petrels. Jill is an archaeologist and, like Stuart, not one to be fanciful. Though she knew most of the Scottish islands, Rona was new to her. It intrigued her because, despite being so remote, as we would say nowadays, when our sense of centre is different, it had been inhabited for centuries. On its south-facing side, there's a long abandoned village surrounded by a swirl of field systems, and a very early Christian chapel. These remains are themselves ancient, but who knows what lay beneath.

Those two, Jill and Stuart, were great observers. Late on the afternoon we arrived, when I'd recovered myself and we'd unpacked all the food and gear, I was out walking, when I caught sight of Stuart in characteristic pose. He was hunkered against an exposed rock that offered views of a cliff loud with guillemots and kittiwakes. He had binoculars in one hand and a notebook pressed open on his knee. I was back at the bothy when he arrived through the heavy door.

'Well?' I said, meaning, how goes the world?
'No' bad.'
'What were you doing?'
'Just having a damn good look.'

'And?'

'Kittiwakes have young, two sometimes.'

'That's good.'

'It *is* good. Maybe it's the start of a recovery. How many gulls have you seen?'

'Me?' I said. 'Gulls? Some. A few.' A few standing on a broken wall, kept a steely eye on us interlopers.

'Exactly. There were near a thousand pairs of Great Black Backs in 2001, chicks running everywhere. They've completely collapsed.'

Then Jill arrived back too, carrying her drawing board. Already she'd been down at the chapel, at the semi-subterranean village where she'd spend much of her time, brushing earth from stones with her strong hands, crawling into passages, shining a torch into gaps unlit for ages.

'Well?' I said again.

That merry smile. 'Ooh, *interesting*.'

'What were you doing?'

'Oh, just... having a look!'

Inhabited once, but now the island is returned to birds and seals; grey seals in thousands breed there, many seemed disinclined to leave. Every day, all around the shore were rocks softened by the shapes of seals; seals watched us from the waters. What we called 'the bothy' was properly a field station for a team of biologists who arrive every November to study the seals at pupping time. The bothy was a green shed, gale-proof and insulated, with two rooms, one with bunks and the other with a kitchen and table, and a container for well water. Every store and roofspace was crammed with equipment and supplies. There were spades and ropes and cupboards of tinned food, and a shelf of fantasy novels and thrillers, which says much about Rona in November. There was even a handwritten copy of Kipling's *If*, pinned to the wall. 'If you can keep your head when all about you / are losing theirs...' But there was little fear of that. Although we were on our own and far from anywhere, Stuart and Jill were both relaxed and robust, old hands at this kind of thing.

That first night sea-sickness and sea air had done for me; come twilight, I dozed in my bunk a couple of hours, but when Jill came and said they were going to the village, I got up again, and like the others, made ready to go out. It was nearly midnight and we went out, because, well, how often do you get the chance to ramble round an uninhabited island, in the northern ocean, in summer – but also, there was something in particular we wanted to witness, which happened only in the darkest hours. Saturday night, and we had a date in town – but instead of glad-rags we pulled on winter waterproofs and hats, because the sea winds were persistent and cold.

The island is only a mile and half long, one fertile hill, two flat near-barren peninsulas, one north, one southwest, like two mismatching wings. There are no beaches, all is cliff, swooping now high, now low, and cut with many geos. The sea prowled into every geo; by night its sound seemed muted, though now and then the breeze brought whoops of seal-song.

Clouds were gathering, but that was good, Stuart said, the darker the better.

We walked westward up a slight rise, which at its crest, gave views down a long slope to the ragged peninsula called Sceapull, which soon surrendered to the waves. A dusty, antique sort of light lay over the island, the sea was the colour of tarnished silver. The path led over a hillside, through a gap in an earthen dyke, whereupon the land began to rise and fall in ridges, like those of a vast scallop shell, waist high ridges between shadow-filled troughs, all with a pelt of long grass that shivered in the wind. The ridges curved downhill toward the sea. Hundreds of years ago oats or barley would have been grown on them, but now, long overgrown, they had become sculptural, land art.

We passed through that strange estate, then arrived at the shell of St Ronan's chapel. Just four stone walls, all speckled with lichen, a low doorway, no roof at all. It faced the southern sea, and dug into the earth between the chapel and the cliffs a quarter mile away were ovals and pockets of darkness, bound by overgrown turf walls – all that remained of the village. Beyond that, beat of the waves.

This was what we'd come for, something faraway and special, so we settled ourselves against the chapel wall to wait.

I think I fell asleep. Half asleep, but started awake because someone had laughed right in my ear. It came again – a stuttery laugh, in the air, a burst of high chatter, sudden as a match-strike. At once it was answered from within the wall itself. A shape tilted fast overhead and Jill beside me said 'look, that's one, they're coming'. Even as she spoke another spat of glee came conjured of the night air; now several dark shapes were darting about the chapel walls, quick like bats but not bats. They chattered as they flew, and from deep within the walls came rapid replies. Jill cast me a laughing look, and as more birds appeared from nowhere, to chase and chatter around us, we could feel the thrum of their wings on our hair.

You have to go a long way to find a breeding colony of Leach's fork-tailed petrels; to a handful of the furthermost islands, St Kilda, the Flannens and here, Rona, where, on summer nights, they make the quick dash ashore. Mate calls mate, *dit-dit diddle-dit!*, rival pursues rival, one partner creeps back into his burrow-nest, allowing the other to be off on her small black wings, far out to sea.

The call, to our human ears, sounded like laughter. At the darkest hour, the walls, like a hive, were busy with birds. They're small as swifts, but their challenge isn't the ocean storms, it's the short race ashore. Great Skuas – Bonxies – prey on them, god knows how, hence their dash by moonlight – except, they prefer no moon. They prefer the darkest of summer nights.

Surf, and seal-song, and petrel glee. By about two o'clock dawn was breathing onto the northeast sky again, and there was an urgent war-time feel in the air, of subterfuge and thrill, and exchanges of the birds' high rapid Morse.

Stuart had been prowling about the village, now he came back, a white-haired figure rounding the chapel end.

'It's wonderful!' I whispered. We stood in the chapel doorway, watching the dark bird-shapes chase above its old walls.

'How far out do they go?'
'Right to the edge of the continental shelf.'
'How far's that?'
'We're about halfway there. Another fifty miles.'

The birds jinked about our heads as we spoke; if they saw or heard us at all they paid no heed.

'Just *magic*!'
'There's no' many..'
'There's loads, look...'
But he shook his head. 'No there's no'.

Leach's petrels are rare and so, under European law, we're supposed to keep a weather eye on them. This was Stuart's task, he'd come to Rona to count their secret nests. He had done the same 10 years ago. Over the next days he'd do it again.

In the morning – though the sun had been high for hours – we again made our way through the fields-systems to the village. The ruins were all innocence by light of day; not a sound came from them, nor from the stones of the chapel. Human presence and retreat was all they admitted to; they denied all knowledge of the night's merriment.

We were blessed with the weather. I had the sensation I always have on Atlantic islands, in summertime, when the clouds pass quickly and light glints on the sea – a sense that the world is bringing itself into being moment by moment. Arising and passing away. Stuart, however, meant business. From a rucksack he produced some bamboo canes and plastic tags. Then he handed me a Sony Walkman.

'Right' he said 'Give three blasts, about thirty seconds, then move on'.

'Where?'

'Anywhere that looks likely.'

Looks likely. We were standing by a curved waist-high wall, that contained an oval space now brightly carpeted with silverweed. Two stones jutted up from the wallhead like praying hands.

'Does that look likely?'

He shrugged. 'Try it'.

I held the tape-recorder to a tiny gap between stone and turf, and pressed the button. The tape whirred, then issued the *dit-dit diddly-dit* of a Leach's petrel, and at once, from under the stones, a muffled but outraged householder *dit diddle-ditted* right back again. It made me laugh, but Stuart wrote a figure on a plastic marker and rammed it into the turf.

'You do the rest of these walls. This'll be your patch, we'll do the village every day. Jill's taking the graveyard. I'll do the chapel dyke.'

'Does it work if you play them Abba?' I asked, but he just gave me a long look.

It was a joy. In sunshine and a businesslike breeze, I made my way around the old walls, pausing every few yards to play the tape and quickly learning the 'likely places'. Some burrows were neat round holes in the turf; the birds dig them out with their feet. If I saw such a burrow, I played the tape, then pressed my ear to the turf. Silence was disappointing, but every time a bird responded from within, it made me laugh again. If a burrow was live, if a bird was tucked inside, there were tiny signs: broken grass stalks, a discrete dropping. You could sometimes smell their peculiar rich musty odour. Some burrows had no visible door, the response came from deep within green tussocks, as if from a fairy boudoir. Now and again the tape elicited some sexy Eartha Kitt purring – that was the female. Only males made the chatterbox call. Sometimes, if one piped up, he set off his neighbours too, so an old turf wall, warming in the sun, started up like a barrel organ.

I found myself saying 'thank you' and 'sorry', and began to feel like a door-to-door salesman, except that, if I looked behind me, there was the ocean, brightly shifting everywhere, meeting the sky in every shade of grey. A little farther uphill, around the chapel, Jill and Stuart worked at their own sections, leaning in to their own walls, as if listening to the heart-beats of stones.

But when we met to compare notes Stuart was again muttering darkly. It was not good, he said. Not like last time. Worrying.

※

Over the next ten days, he covered the entire island, from the lighthouse at the eastern cliff-top, down to the ends of both storm-scoured peninsulas. Sometimes Jill and I helped. We laid blue nylon ropes over the ground to mark off strips of land, so we could tell where we'd been when every stone began to look identical. Within the ropes, we crawled a few yards apart, playing our tapes under rocks and cairns. Sometimes birds answered, and soon I couldn't see an unexplored rock without my heart giving a little leap – a likely place! We found bits of birds, a cradle of seals' ribs, the exquisite skeleton of a starfish, no bigger than a thumbnail. It was a curious task, very intimate, to sail to a faraway island, then crawl over it on hands and knees, like pilgrims or penitents.

Every morning we worked the village, which held by far the greatest concentration of birds, and soon developed a feel

for the colony's dynamic. If a bird who'd replied every day
for three days was suddenly absent, he got a cross against his
number in my notebook, and I knew that he'd slipped out to
sea in the small hours. Gone from the chapel, from the village.
A wing and a prayer. Now his mate would be sitting meekly
on her single egg, a dark eye in the darkness within the dyke.

While Stuart spoke to the birds, Jill communed with stones.
First she concentrated on St Ronan's chapel. It's just a shell now,
the stones of its western gable much collapsed. It stands at the
southern wall of an enclosure, and within the enclosure is a
little graveyard, very old. The turf has risen over the centuries,
so the humble gravestones, hewn of the sparkly island feldspar,
tilt this way and that like little sinking ships.

Nothing is known of St Ronan but his name, which, oddly,
means 'little seal' – as if he'd been a Rona selkie who'd swopped
his seal skin for the habit of a monk. Doubtless he was one of the
early Scots-Irish monks, who sailed from his monastery to seek
'a desert place in the sea', where he could live a life of austerity
and prayer. Hundreds of years later, the people built the chapel
in his name, and buried their dead beside it. Now those people
are gone too, their graveyard is a poignant place.

But suddenly it was *en fête*. This was Jill's doing. One
day she went around the graveyard and festooned it with a
little orange flags on wires, one beside every stone, and the
flags snapped in the breeze, so the cemetery seemed to be
celebrating a day of the dead. She was plotting the grave markers
on a chart; the yellow flags helped her see them as she measured
their distance from a baseline: a measuring tape strung across
the enclosure wall to wall. She was doing this because the stones
were going missing. By studying black and white photographs
from the 1930s or '50s she could tell that the stone crosses were
being quietly stolen away and, by dint of wind and weather,
the medieval chapel was ever more collapsed. It troubled her.

The chapel, village and all the surrounding fields are a Scheduled Ancient Monument, in the care of the state, but the state is far away and has more pressing concerns. So Jill said, 'we can at least plot them, so there's a record of what there was.' Really, she'd like to get people out here, experts from official agencies, an architect, or a drystone dyker, who could do some discrete shoring up and save the chapel from complete ruination.

One bright afternoon I held measuring poles and called out the numbers she needed, while Jill, a black baseball-cap pulled over her thick hair, bent over a board and mapped the people's graves.

Of course it made us think of them. The long dead people whose graves we knelt on. We called them 'them' and spoke about them every day. How did they live, what were their lives like, people who'd managed for generations, out here alone in the sea?

The Rona people weren't unique, they were Gaels; part of the wider culture of the Western Isles and, as Jill kept reminding us, the sea then was a conduit, not a barrier. Nonetheless they lived a long way from any neighbours, had to fend for themselves, with their fields and few cattle and sea birds' eggs. But by the time Martin Martin wrote his travel journal of the Western Isles, in 1695, the people were already gone. 'That ancient race', he called them, 'perfectly ignorant of most of those vices that abound in the world', and, when you wander round their village and look out at the uninterrupted sea, you know why.

Ronan's name is known, but the names of those buried under the turf are lost, save for one tantalising detail, which Martin gives. The Rona people, he says, 'took their surname from the colour of the sky, rainbow and clouds.'

'Such *work*', Jill would say, as we strolled through the overgrown fields. When I asked her who had first come to Rona, if it were Neolithic or Bronze Age people or what, she just smiled and said, 'Ooh, we don't know, do we?' The sea may have been the highway then, but it was still a long way to venture in a dug-out boat.

The work indeed. All those acres of undulating fields, built up by hand of the scant earth and seaweed. Outside the enclosing dyke, lay the rest of the island, not a mile and a half long, which the people must have known down to every blade of grass, every stone. They must have felt acutely the turning of the seasons, the need to lay down stores and supplies, because summer was fleeting. We arrived in early July, when bog cotton was in bloom, soft white tufts facing into the wind. Two weeks later, its seeds clung to rocks and grasses, or were out to sea and lost.

Daily, our sense of time slowed, days expanded like a wing. The days were long in the best, high-summer sense; at night we put up storm shutters on the bothy to make it dark enough to sleep. Time was clouds passing, a sudden squall, a shift in the wind. Often we wondered what it would do to your mind if you were born here, and lived your whole life within this small compass. To be named for the sky or the rainbow, and live in constant sight and sound of the sea. After a mere fortnight I felt lighter inside, as though my bones were turning to flutes.

St Ronan rode to Rona on the back of a sea-monster, so the legend says. Monster or boat, he'd have jumped ashore giving prayers of thanks, sometime in the eighth century.

Whether he was really alone, as romanticists would have it, or whether others came with him – monks, lay penitents, men without women, – well, as Jill would say, we don't know, do we? Surely it would have taken more than one to do the spadework; even saints must eat. And if there were people on Rona already, watching as the Christians' boat drew nearer – we don't know that either.

But we know what the saint sought, because on Rona – too far away to have been bothered with, to have been destroyed by Reformation zeal, there survives something unique. It's within the chapel, and is entered through a square of darkness low on the eastern gable, a portal with a lintel of white quartz, as though it were Neolithic. You have to crawl to enter, but once inside you can stand freely. At first it seems wholly dark, and it smells of damp earth, but as your eyes adjust, stars of daylight begin to spangle here and there overhead, where, over the many centuries, the stones have slipped a little; so after a while, it's like being in a wild planetarium.

Darkness, earth... and a sudden quiet: no wind or surf; you find yourself in a place from which all the distracting world is banned. Then you see the stonework. It is beautifully made, and has stood for 1,200 years. A low stone altar stands against the east wall. So there is one thing we know of the saint – he had a feel for stone; strong hands. Or someone did. This is what he made for himself; having sailed to this island of sea-light and sky and seals and crying birds – a world-denying cell.

Two or three times, when Stuart was inquiring of the birds, and Jill of stones, I crept into the oratory, and waited till my eyes adjusted to the low light. I went warily, because a fulmar had made her nest in a corner; too close and she'd spit. A fulmar guarding the saint's cell, and it was strange to think there were Leach's petrels secreted in the walls. Petrels, named for St Peter, who walked on water, had colonised a cell built by a saint named for a seal.

I crept in just to wonder what he did in there, Ronan; to imagine him right there, in front of the altar, wrapped in darkness, rapt in prayer, closed off from the sensory world, the better to connect with – what?

⁂

I say we had the island to ourselves, but of course that's nonsense. There were the seals, and thousands of puffins, and colonies of terns on the low rocks, forever rising against some fresh outrage, and down among the rock-pools, shags' slatternly nests.

One evening six swifts appeared, circled above the bothy and then vanished again. A party of Risso's dolphins arrived out of the blue, spent half an hour feeding just off the south side, then they too went on their way. The time of thrift had passed; every day we met a flock of crossbills, of all things, which twittered round the island, feeding on thrift seeds. Crossbills are birds of the northern pine forest, but nary a pine tree here, and long sea miles to travel before they saw one again. There were about a hundred; the males were bright red, and the females brown, so when they all flew by, they were like embers blown from a bonfire.

And although no inhabited land was in sight, we weren't even truly alone in the ocean. Ten miles west, like the moon to Rona's fertile earth, rose the barren rock of Sula Sgeir, – a gannet factory. And there was always the sense of the 'ancient race'. Personally, if ever I felt remote or cut off, it wasn't from the mainland far over the horizon, but from the abandoned village a quarter mile away. There was something sweetly domestic and recognizable about those few rickles of stones, the humble chapel. We ate packet soups and tinned fruit, looking through the window at the relics of a lost intelligence, the long-forsaken fields, gilded in evening light.

Cleared of dishes of an evening the bothy table accumulated notebooks and bird reports, archaeological monographs, plans and photographs. One evening, maybe a week after we'd arrived, Stuart was sitting opposite Jill and me, head bowed, noting figures and tapping a calculator, calibrating the figures his field work was producing. He'd covered about half the island with his tapes. Abruptly he said, 'there's some consistency emerging here. Almost 40% decline, I think, all over. And very suddenly.'

We paused. We all loved the Leach's petrels: their midnight flit, the back-chat they gave us from their burrows.

'That's bad.' said Jill.

'Why though?' I asked, but Stuart didn't answer.

'Maybe they get eaten…' Jill said, but he shook his head. 'I'm sure it's not predators. Bonxies get the blame but I'm sure its not just that.'

'What then?' Again he shook his head.

'But you must have some idea' I persisted. ' 'Is it to do with climate change, with the ocean; is there not enough food? What *do* they eat, anyway?'

'Zooplankton, larval-stage fish… creepy-crawly things…'

'Plankton? We're not running out of plankton, are we?'

This time Stuart put down his pencil, took off his glasses and pinched his eyes.

'I *don't know*. But *something's* going on out there.'

※

Stuart often said there was no such thing as 'natural harmony'. It was a dynamic. Populations expand, then crash. Mysterious things happen; catastrophic things sometimes, on the island, everywhere. Nothing stays the same.

Our attitude to the village houses we explored and the fields we walked was tempered by a particular piece of knowledge, this: the Rona people hadn't simply quit their tenancy and sailed away to a life less isolated. Neither had they been forcibly cleared. The village was abandoned because the people had died, all wiped out, suddenly.

It happened about 1680. Their fate was discovered because of a shipwreck. A man called McLeod, his wife and a 'good crew' were heading home from St Kilda to Harris, but a storm blew up which drove them a hundred miles north until they were cast up on the rocks of Rona. They managed to save themselves and some provisions, but their boat was destroyed. They'd have been hoping for help, but what they found were corpses.

What had happened is unsure, the stories are peculiar. A plague of rats had somehow swarmed ashore, and devoured the people's supplies. Pirates had stolen their bull. No boat had come north from Lewis that year, which might have brought supplies. These calamities, compounded, were too much. But with everyone dead, who was left to bear witness?

The shipwrecked party buried the bodies, and overwintered, and in Spring, fashioned a new boat which they sailed home to Harris, to arrive like revenants. That was then. No-one has really lived on Rona since.

※

'Come and look at this stonework', said Jill, on our next to last day.

She led us through the village to its southern edge toward some more curved low walls, built, as were all the dwelling houses, of stone and turf. To my untrained eye the walls looked no different to the others, but Jill beckoned us to follow her as she jumped down into a curving sort of trench. Then she kneeled at the entrance of a short passageway about four feet long. There, she brushed the side wall with her hand. Its stones were close-packed and neat.

'See how different this stonework is to the rest, how thick? This wall's about three-feet thick. Solid. But now, come and look here.'

From the doorway, she followed the external wall a few yards rightward, to a place where it had partially collapsed. There was a hole just big enough to peer into. She handed over her torch and told us to look through the gap. It was like spying through a letterbox into a hallway beyond.

'It's hollow!'

'Caved in, I think.' She took the torch herself and shone the light into the gap within the wall, so the light played along a particular stone, which was tilted with one end in the earth.

'See that stone? If that's a lintel, and if all that stuff that looks like a floor is actually accumulation debris, then we're looking at a passageway enclosed within two walls. Now come up here...'

She climbed nimbly up onto the wallhead and stood above us on an uneven platform of flat stones.

'This is its roof, a bit caved in...'

'You're standing on the roof...?'

'... of a cell-like structure. Which is a side chamber to that bigger interior, the one that first passageway entered into. This chamber is contained within the thickness of the wall. Maybe it was a sleeping area. All of this' – she gestured around her – 'was a very thick-walled circular structure...'

'That means it's old?'

'Ooh, two thousand years? But what's happened is that new people have come and changed it to suit themselves. So, jump down here again, come inside... and you have a rectangular room, cut into the pre-existing round structure, see? This was done much, much later... look how the stonework here's not very well made, really, compared to where we just were...'

'Two thousand years? You mean when the Christians came, there was already a thousand years of settlement... ?'

Jill smiled. 'Could have been people here, or they could have come and gone... more than once.'

'Long periods of abandonment...?'

'Maybe centuries...'

'Perhaps that's what this is.' I said, meaning that perhaps some day in the future, when change unimaginable has come, a few acres far out in the Atlantic might be pressed into service again.

※

Tonight, at home, with the blinds closed against winter dark, I wonder what Rona is like right now. The Leach's petrels, new colonisers of the village, will be away far down into the

Southern Atlantic. The cliffs will be empty too, the puffins and guillemots dispersed out to sea. Skuas also, all headed south. As for the crossbills, heaven knows. One day they must simply have upped sticks and gone, all at once, twittering over the waves.

As I write the shipping forecast gives '... increasing severe gale force nine later', but that's nothing. Some storm waves are so big they sweep clean over the peninsula of Fianius. I'd like to witness Rona in winter – short terse days, the sea roar, nights under the wheel of the stars. You'd soon find out why the houses were dug down into the insulating earth.

Many people, including the Stornoway coastguard, knew we were on Rona, and we had radios, but still, that last morning, as we cleared the bothy and prepared to leave, we all three kept glancing at the horizon. Nothing was said, but only when the boat appeared, a steady gleam in the south east, did we relax. When it did, that was our signal. The wind was rising, the skipper wouldn't want to hang about, so we began to heft all the sea bags, sleeping bags, gas bottles, tape recorders and notebooks back down the hillside to the geo, where black rocks tilted to the waves.

Author Biographies

Elisabeth Bletsoe was born near Wimborne in Dorset. She has degrees in psychology and history. Her works include *The Regardians*, *Portraits of the Artist's Sister*, *Pharmacopoeia*, *Landscape from a Dream* and *Pharmacopoeia & Early Selected Works*. She has appeared in the anthologies *Earth Ascending* and *Infinite Difference* and will also feature in the forthcoming Shearsman Books anthology of radical landscape poetry, *The Ground Aslant*. Elisabeth's work has also been broadcast on Resonance FM and Radio 3's *The Verb*. Since 1997 she has been involved with administration, conservation and research at Sherborne Museum. A lifelong student of plants and plant medicine, she has recently completed a biographical work on the Edwardian botanical artist Diana Ruth Wilson.

Lavinia Greenlaw was born in London, where she has lived for most of her life. Her most recent book of poems is *Minsk* (2003) and her fourth collection, *The Casual Perfect*, will appear in Spring 2011. Her other books include two novels, *Mary George of Allnorthover* and *An Irresponsible Age*, a collaboration with Garry Fabian Miller, *Thoughts of a Night Sea*, and *The Importance of Music to Girls*. She has won several awards, including a NESTA Fellowship, and has held residencies at the Science Museum and the Royal Society of Medicine. Her work for BBC radio includes programmes about the Arctic and the Baltic, Emily Dickinson, Elizabeth Bishop and Dutch landscape painting. She has also written radio drama and opera libretti. She is Professor of Creative Writing at the University of East Anglia.

Jay Griffiths is a British writer living in Wales, and author of *Pip Pip: A Sideways Look at Time*, *Anarchipelago* and *Wild: An Elemental Journey*. A winner of the Barnes & Noble Discover Award for the best new non-fiction writer to be published in the USA, as well as the inaugural Orion Book

Award in 2007, she has also been shortlisted for both the Orwell prize and for the World Book Day Award. She contributes regularly to *The Idler* and *Orion*.

Kathleen Jamie was born in the west of Scotland. Her most recent poetry collection, *The Tree House,* won both the Forward Poetry Prize and the Scottish Book of the Year Award. In 2005 a non-fiction book, *Findings*, appeared to great acclaim. Kathleen is Professor of Creative Writing at Stirling University. She lives with her family in Fife.

Richard Mabey is the author of more than thirty books, among them *Flora Britannica*, which won the British Book Awards' Illustrated Book of the Year, and *Nature Cure*. He writes a regular column for *BBC Wildlife* magazine and on nature for *The Times*, *The Guardian* and *Granta*. His latest book is *Weeds: How Vagabond Plants Gatecrashed Civilisation and Changed the Way We Think about Nature*. He lives in Norfolk.

Robert Macfarlane is the author of *Mountains of the Mind* (Granta, 2003) and *The Wild Places* (Granta, 2007). He is currently completing a book called *The Old Ways*, about paths, tracks, stories and thought. He is a Fellow of Emmanuel College, Cambridge.

Alice Oswald trained as a gardener. She has published five collections of poetry and two anthologies.

Jane Rendell is Director of Architectural Research at the Bartlett, UCL. An architectural designer and historian, art critic and writer, her work has explored various inter-disciplinary intersections: feminist theory and architectural history, fine art and architectural design, autobiographical writing and criticism. She is the author of *Site-Writing*, *Art and Architecture* and *The Pursuit of Pleasure* and co-editor of *Pattern*, *Critical Architecture*, *Spatial Imagination*, *The*

Unknown City, *Intersections*, *Gender Space Architecture* and *Strangely Familiar*.

Robin Robertson is from the north-east coast of Scotland. His fourth collection, *The Wrecking Light*, was published earlier this year and his translation of *Medea* has recently been dramatised for stage and radio. He has received the E.M. Forster Award from the American Academy of Arts and Letters and all three Forward Poetry Prizes.

Iain Sinclair has lived in (and written about) Hackney, London, since 1969. His novels include *Downriver* (Winner of the James Tait Black Prize & the Encore Prize for the Year's Best Second Novel), *Radon Daughters*, *Landor's Tower* and, most recently, *Dining on Stones* (which was shortlisted for the Ondaatje Prize). Non-fiction books, exploring the myth and matter of London, include *Lights Out for the Territory*, *London Orbital* and *Edge of the Orison*. In the '90s Iain wrote and presented a number of films for BBC2's Late Show and has, subsequently, co-directed with Chris Petit four documentaries for Channel 4; one of which, *Asylum*, won the short film prize at the Montreal Film Festival. He edited *London, City of Disappearances* and his most recent book is *Hackney, That Rose-Red Empire*, published in February 2009.

Ken Worpole has written books on architecture, literature, landscape and social policy. He was a member of the UK government Urban Green Spaces Task Force, an Adviser to the Commission for Architecture and the Built Environment (CABE), and was recently appointed a Senior Professor in the Cities Institute at London Metropolitan University. His books include *Here Comes the Sun: Architecture and Public Space in 20th Century European Culture* (2001); *Last Landscapes: The Architecture of the Cemetery in the West* (2003); *350 Miles: An Essex Journey*, with photographer Jason Orton (2005) and, most recently, *Modern Hospice Design: The Architecture of Palliative Care* (2009). He has lived in Hackney for the past forty years with his wife, the photographer Larraine Worpole, and is currently working on a book on the future of public libraries.

Editor Biographies

Gareth Evans works as an independent moving image/event curator, editor and writer. He edited the international moving image journal *Vertigo* and now co-edits the new cross arts magazine *Artesian* (www.gotogetherpress.com). He has conceived and curated many international film seasons and festivals including the major season *John Berger: Here Is Where We Meet* (www.johnberger.org; 2005) and *All Power to the Imagination! 1968 and Its Legacies* (2008).

Di Robson is an independent cultural producer, consultant and lecturer, working nationally and internationally. Current contracts include the production of the 2012 event in Exhibition Road for The Royal Borough of Kensington and Chelsea. She has produced and/or programmed a wide range of festivals and events including *John Berger: Here Is Where We Meet* (2005) and the *Jaipur Heritage International Festival* (2003–06). Di has worked extensively in experimental performance, is a mentor on a number of programmes, amongst them Space 11 in Glasgow and the Roundhouse, London. She was the Consultant Producer of *SPILL Festival*, London 2007.

Chapter Opening Images

p. 8: Robin Robertson
p. 12: Oona Grimes
p. 28: Adam Shawyer (*Norfolk. The Broads. View South West from Breydon Water towards Halvergate Marshes*)
p. 40: Jane Rendell ('Moss Green', 2001)
pp. 42–49: Found images
p. 60: Jason Orton
p. 82: Frances Hatch (*Cloud Piercing: Charmouth*)
p. 90: Alice Smith
p. 104: Garry Fabian Miller (*Year Two, Growen I*, June 2007. Oil, light, dye destruction print. Courtesy HackelBury Fine Art, London)
p. 106: Nick Hayes
p. 132: Tarka Kings
p. 134: Stuart Murray

Acknowledgements

Thank you to all our writers and artists for their exceptional contributions, and to all at Fraser Muggeridge studio. Many thanks also to Chenine Bhathena, Jason Bowman, Régis Cochefert, Ariane Koek, Sukhdev Sandhu, Lyndy Stout and Kate Tyndall. *The Re-Enchantment* would not have been possible without the support of the Paul Hamlyn Foundation. Niloufer Sagar of Artevents continues to render herself invaluable. Finally, personal thanks from Di to Tony Guilfoyle and Gareth to Tereza Stehlíková, for their ongoing support, encouragement, patience and love.

Artevents is a production agency, co-directed by Gareth Evans and Di Robson, that provides a platform for artists to explore the nature and values of contemporary society through extended artistic intervention.

Also published and edited by Artevents (and available via the website): *John Berger, a Season in London*, 2005.

www.artevents.info